THE
Bible
FROM
Scratch

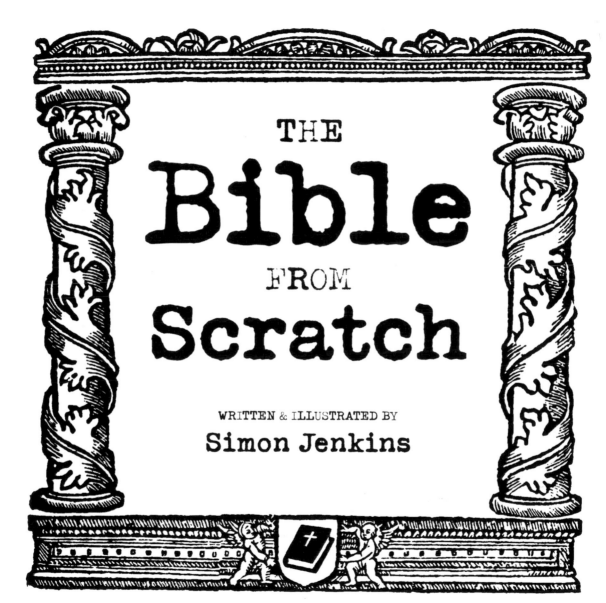

THE

Bible

FROM

Scratch

WRITTEN & ILLUSTRATED BY

Simon Jenkins

The publishing team included Brian Singer-Towns, development editor; Gary Dreier and Lorraine Kilmartin, reviewers; prepress and manufacturing coordinated by the prepublication and production services departments of Saint Mary's Press.

Printed in the United States of America

4326

ISBN 978-0-88489-940-2

Acknowledgments

Scripture quotations from the Good News Bible published by The Bible Societies/ HarperCollins Publishers, copyright © 1966, 1971, 1976, 1992 American Bible Society.

Scripture quotations from the Holy Bible, New International Version, copyright © 1973, 1978, 1984 International Bible Society. Used by permission of Zondervan and Hodder & Stoughton Limited. All rights reserved. The "NIV" and "New International Version" trademarks are registered in the United States Patent and Trademark Office by International Bible Society. Use of either trademark requires the permission of International Bible Society. UK trademark number 1448790

The Scripture quotations contained herein are from the New Revised Standard Version Bible: Catholic Edition copyright © 1993 and 1989 by the Division of Christian Education of the National Council of the Churches of Christ in the U.S.A. All rights reserved."

Illustration of Martin Luther King on p. 129 by David Jackson, and image of Jesus of p. 206 used by permission of the Churches Advertising Network.

What's this?

What's this? The Bible explained in cartoons? Whatever would Moses say? Or Habakkuk? Would Elijah have burned it? And would Paul turn in his catacomb to see his life's work reduced to a few scribbles?

Hopefully not. The Bible's characters themselves weren't shy about using different methods of communication to get across what they had to say. Jeremiah smashed crockery. Ezekiel performed weird, one-man plays. David sang songs. Nathan told a trick story. Jesus talked in pictures.

And this drive to popularize has sometimes surfaced in the history of the church, too. St Augustine, heavyweight theologian though he was, took time out to compose pop songs to attack the heretics. And John Calvin, no less, wrote Christian lyrics to Genevan jigs.

This book is humbly offered in the same spirit. It's intended as a beginner's guide to the Good Book, something to help readers start their own explorations in the Bible.

Some thank yous are due: first, to Talitha, my daughter, for keying in all the handwritten text from the original 1987 edition of the book. Also to Nathan, my son, for making the graffiti graphic on page 108. And to Steve Tomkins, for reading the original text and making both serious and mischievous suggestions for improving it.

I also owe a debt of love and gratitude to David Alexander, whose creativity and encouragement during my time as an editor at Lion Publishing brought this book into being.

Simon Jenkins

Inside the Bible from Scratch

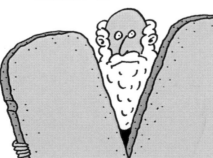

Jesus

Not just one, but four versions of the life of Jesus, as told by Matthew, Mark, Luke and John

The Church

The message of Jesus travels from Jerusalem to Rome in the space of a single book – the book of Acts

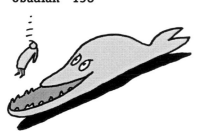

Letters

Intercepted mail from the first Christian churches, complete with revealing, embarrassing and inspiring moments

The End

The Bible's showstopping ending, with trumpets, giant choirs, the curtain drawn back on heaven, and every tear wiped away

Big, black book

Once upon a time, the Bible was a big black book with golden-edged pages that required a course in bodybuilding before you could lift it off the shelf.

In recent times, though, the Bible's been repackaged and has sunsets and puppy dogs and other marketing-friendly pictures on the cover, and no longer weighs a ton. But even though it now looks like any other bestseller, the Bible still stands out as being a book unlike any other.

For a start, it was produced by two of the world's big faiths: Judaism and Christianity. You can see this in the way the Bible is structured into two "halves": the Old Testament and the New Testament. The Old half contains the scriptures (holy writings), of Judaism, while Christians regard both Old and New as their scriptures.

The word "testament" means "agreement". The Bible's first half centers on the agreement God made with Moses and Israel at Mt Sinai, and the second half on the agreement God made available to all people through the death of Jesus Christ. The Old Testament contains 46 books, while the New Testament is smaller, with 27 books.

On top of that, a third world faith – Islam – also regards the Bible as a holy book, although Muslims believe that the Bible has been corrupted and is inferior to the Qu'ran.

Books, chapters and verses

When you buy a Bible, you're not buying just one book, you're buying 73 books rolled into one. Take a look at the contents page of the Bible, and you'll find all 73 books listed, some with names that give a clue to what they're about, such as Kings, Song of Solomon and Revelation, but most with the names of the people said to have written them, such as Matthew, Mark, Luke and John.

The Bible was divided into chapters in the 13th century by Stephen Langton, who went on to become Archbishop of Canterbury. It was only broken down into verses after the invention of printing.

Robert Stephanus created the verses of the New Testament in the 1550s, and legend has it that he chopped it all up while riding on horseback between Paris and Lyon... which may explain why some of the breaks happen in unexpected places.

These books were written, edited and collected into the thick volume we know as the Bible over about 1,500 years. During that time, all sorts of material was gathered together: songs, legal contracts, letters, stories, riddles, official histories, poems, family trees and so on. This makes the Bible like a huge warehouse with a vast variety of curious and compelling bits and pieces hidden away on its shelves.

The chart opposite shows how these different materials are structured in the Bible.

Weighing in at close to a million words, the Bible can seem like a daunting read. But as well as being broken down into two testaments and 73 books, each book is broken down into chapters, and each chapter into verses of a sentence or two each. All of which helps you feel you're actually getting somewhere when you start reading it.

Ancient blockbuster

The Bible also stands out for its enduring popularity. Have you ever thought how curious it is that the Bible is still such a bestselling and much-read book? The ink on the pages of the Bible has been dry for almost 2,000 years – that's when the last writer laid down his pen – and yet it's still being read all over the world today. By any terms, that's a huge achievement.

In the last 150 years alone, an estimated 1.6 billion Bibles have been printed. And it's been translated into no fewer than 3,000 languages.

Just think about it. This is an ancient book. How many people go out and buy 2,000-year-old texts from the ancient world for their reading pleasure? ... Sophocles, Plato, the Epic of Gilgamesh, Plutarch, Livy, Ovid... Anyone for Euripides?

How the Bible fits together

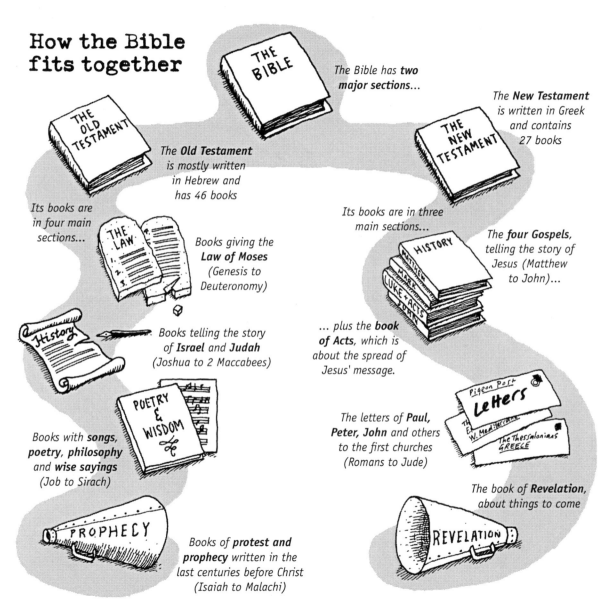

The Bible has **two major sections...**

The **Old Testament** is mostly written in Hebrew and has 46 books

The **New Testament** is written in Greek and contains 27 books

Its books are in four main sections...

THE LAW

Books giving the **Law of Moses** (Genesis to Deuteronomy)

History

Books telling the story of **Israel** and **Judah** (Joshua to 2 Maccabees)

POETRY & WISDOM

Books with **songs, poetry, philosophy** and **wise sayings** (Job to Sirach)

PROPHECY

Books of **protest and prophecy** written in the last centuries before Christ (Isaiah to Malachi)

Its books are in three main sections...

HISTORY

The **four Gospels**, telling the story of Jesus (Matthew to John)...

... plus the **book of Acts**, which is about the spread of Jesus' message.

Letters

The letters of **Paul, Peter, John** and others to the first churches (Romans to Jude)

REVELATION

The book of **Revelation**, about things to come

Things were different in the days of the Bible... for example, the haircuts...

Hmm... can you do something with the side bits?

And the Bible isn't just ancient, it's oriental. It's not a modern, western book. That's why it can sound foreign to us at first reading. It's full of details such as what to do if you get mildew on your tent flap, how to carry out the interior design of a temple, or the best way to handle a runaway slave.

But even though this book comes to us out of the distant past, it still makes compulsive reading. Part of the reason is that we can see our reflection in the book's characters and stories. This is part of the Bible's power – its stories speak to us. It's one of the reasons why we break the habit of a lifetime and read a 2,000-year-old book.

The Bible is a book that is endlessly retold – especially by being translated into new languages. Aside from the huge translation projects that have brought the Good Book to remote tribespeople around the world, the most famous bits of the Bible have also been "translated" for Cockneys, black rappers, Glaswegians, and even extraterrestrials such as the Klingons.

Here's the creation of heaven and earth from Genesis chapter 1, according to *The Black Bible Chronicles*, a 'hip and holy' version written for the streets of the South Bronx...

Now when the Almighty was first down with His program, He made the heavens and the earth. The earth was a fashion misfit, being so uncool and dark, but the Spirit of the Almighty came down real tough, so that He simply said, 'Lighten up!'

And here's the same passage in *A Glasgow Bible*...

It wis a lang time ago, right enough – thoosans an thoosans o years since. There wis nuthin whaur the earth is the noo – absolutely nuthin at aw.

'Weell noo,' God says tae himsel wan day, **'I'll fix a
wee bit dod o land – doon there.'**

Meanwhile, one of the gentlest and best-loved passages from the
Old Testament is now available to the most bloodthirsty beings
in our neck of the Galaxy – the Klingons. Psalm 23 ('The Lord is
my shepherd'), brought to us courtesy of the Klingon Language
Institute, begins...

QorghwI'wI' ghaH joH'a''e' jIHvaD Dach pagh.

For those not fluent in Klingon, this roughly translates as
'Caretaker-my he-is great-lord, for-me it-lacks nothing.'

God and his ghost-writers

The true focus of the Bible's power is not just its ability to
tell a good story, or last forever as a bestseller, or engage our
imagination. Its power lies somewhere else. And it's this: the Bible
shows us God. This isn't just any old book. Christians believe the
73 books of the Bible are uniquely the word of God: that is, God
speaks to us through them and shows us what kind of God he is.

Christians believe the Bible is the revelation of God. They say
we can't discover the truth about God simply by thinking hard
or long enough. We can only know God when he makes the first
move. God reveals himself most fully to us in the coming of Jesus
into the world, and the written word of God, the Bible, is part of
that revelation.

The Catholic Church puts it this way, in a teaching document
called *Dei Verbum* (or Divine Revelation): "The books of Scripture
firmly, faithfully and without error teach that truth which God,
for the sake of our salvation, wished to see confided to the
Sacred Scriptures."

How does God do this? One word the Bible uses to describe the "how" of revelation is the word *inspired*. Here's the famous quotation which is often used when people talk about the God-given status of the Bible...

All scripture is inspired by God and is useful for teaching, for reproof, for correction, and for training in righteousness, so that everyone who belongs to God may be proficient, equipped for every good work.

2 Timothy 3:16

The Greek word used here for "inspired" literally means "God-breathed". Scripture is God breathing out. Just as when we speak, we are breathing out, so God breathes out his word from the depths of his being. This implies that the Bible has its origins in God himself.

Here's another famous quotation about God and inspiration...

The Greek word for "inspired" is theopneustos: theo = "God" and pneustos = "breathed". We get the word "pneumatic" from the same Greek word, as in pneumatic tires on cars and bikes.

Prophecy never had its origin in the will of man...

(that is, it wasn't people making theories about God)

... but men spoke from God as they were carried along by the Holy Spirit.

2 Peter 1:21

The Greek word for "carried along" is the same word that is used to talk about a sailing ship being blown along by the wind. There's the same idea of breath or wind here.

These verses, plus others in the Bible, lead Christians to believe that the writers of the Bible were moved by God's Spirit, so that what they wrote was inspired by God. That's why many Christians look at the Bible as a key authority for what they believe and how they should live.

These descriptions work well in talking about the experience of the most striking characters in the Old Testament – people such as Moses or Elijah, who received direct revelations from God. Here's Jeremiah, for example, one of the greatest prophets...

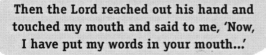

Then the Lord reached out his hand and touched my mouth and said to me, 'Now, I have put my words in your mouth...'

Jeremiah 1:9

And here's Ezekiel, in his famous-but-bizarre vision of the valley of dry bones...

Then the Lord said to me, "Prophesy to these bones and say to them, 'Dry bones! Hear the word of the Lord!'"

Ezekiel 37:4

In these examples, God breaks in like a radio message and tells the prophet what to say. Many writers in the early days of the church looked at verses such as these and talked about the Bible's

*How it didn't happen...
remote-controlled
prophets*

writers being like musical instruments played by the Spirit. The instruments might be human, but the music was perfect and was God's.

Other Christian writers haven't been so happy with that picture of God strumming his guitar or tootling his flute, as it suggests the prophets were completely passive, and maybe even possessed, when they gave their prophecies. To change the image, it's as if God was holding the remote control and the prophet had no say in what was happening.

Most Christian commentators have resisted the idea that the Bible was dictated by God, or handed down from a passing cloud. They've balanced the divine side of the Bible by also stressing its human side – that it was written by real, messy human beings. In the past century, Christians have talked more about the human writers of the Bible and have come to appreciate and even enjoy the fact that because they were human beings, their likes and dislikes, their sense of humor and even their bad grammar comes across in what they wrote.

Just as Christians believe Jesus was fully God and fully a human being, so the Bible is inspired by God but is also a human production. It didn't drop out of heaven one day. God's inspiration had to negotiate with the very imperfect characters of David, Mark, Solomon, Paul and the other writers.

Even though the Bible has plenty of instances of prophets being told, 'Hit them with this!' by God, there are huge stretches of the book where this just doesn't happen. Large chunks of the Bible don't have any dramatic, supernatural revelations, in which people hear voices from heaven, or get told what to say, or see fantastic visions.

Take the book of Esther, for instance, which in some versions doesn't even mention the word "God". Or the hundreds of wise sayings and riddles in the book of Proverbs. Or the long family tree which takes up most of the first chapter of Matthew's Gospel. What about these writings? Were they "breathed out" by God – and if so, how were the writers inspired?

Some Christian thinkers have suggested that God's Spirit was flexible in the way he inspired the Bible's different writers. He might have spoken a direct word in the ear of a prophet, they say, but for King Solomon, the Spirit gave him such a strong dose of wisdom that his proverbs were what God wanted to be said. Or in the case of Luke, who carefully collected and researched the story of Jesus, Christian thinkers have argued that the Holy Spirit guided the process so that Luke's Gospel is the word not just of Luke, but of God, too.

So is it true?

How much can we trust the Bible? Can we believe in what it says? Is it possible the Bible contains mistakes, and if so, what does that do to our faith? Do Christians have to accept everything happened just as it says - even the stories which seem a bit implausible - or is there some room for negotiation?

Some Christians believe the Bible is 100 percent free from errors of any kind, saying every single word in the original manuscripts was inspired by God. As one preacher put it: "God said it, that settles it, I believe it!" For many people who hold this view, God created the world in six, 24-hour days, because that is what they read straight off the page in Genesis chapter 1.

This view of the Bible has been hugely popular among some Christians around the world. In its most extreme form, it is

The prize for the strangest and yet most precise dating of the moment of creation goes to Archbishop James Ussher, Anglican Primate of Ireland. In 1650, he declared that his calculations showed the creation to have happened at 12 noon on 23 October 4004 BC. This was based partly on counting the 'begats' in the Bible and on a symbolic numbering scheme.

antagonistic to the findings of modern science, and Charles Darwin in particular. This is the view which comes closest to saying the human writers of the Bible were mere keyboards which God used to key in the messages he wanted, word for word.

Catholic Christians, along with many others, are cautious about claiming the Bible is literally true, word for word. The Catholic church has some important things to say about the truth of the scriptures. The following points are taken from *Dei Verbum* ("The Word of God"), a major teaching document of the Second Vatican Council.

1. The essentials – the church says the Bible is without error when it talks about the truths God has revealed for our salvation. Here are the words of *Dei Verbum*...

Since everything asserted by the inspired authors or sacred writers must be held to be asserted by the Holy Spirit, it follows that the books of Scripture must be acknowledged as teaching solidly, faithfully and without error that truth which God wanted put into sacred writings.

2. Interpreting wisely – when reading different parts of the Bible, it's important to remember what kind of writing we're looking at. Some of the writers are recounting history, while others are detailing family trees, setting out law codes, writing poetry, giving prophesy or penning a letter to friends. These types of writing are different, and they need different ways of reading, too. So when a poet says...

He who dwells in the shelter of the Most High will rest in the shadow of the Almighty.
Psalm 91:1

... it doesn't mean that God literally casts a shadow on the ground! We need to read poetry as poetry and understand how it uses metaphors and images. As Dei Verbum says...

For the correct understanding of what the sacred author wanted to assert, due attention must be paid to the customary and characteristic styles of feeling, speaking and narrating which prevailed at the time of the sacred writer, and to the patterns men normally employed at that period in their everyday dealings with one another.

We also need to understand that our modern eyes are looking at an ancient text. The biblical writers had a very different understanding of science, and their culture was very different from ours, too. This means that what looks to us like a mistake in the Bible is sometimes down to the writer's different understanding of science, history or culture. Hopefully, *The Bible from Scratch* will help explain some of the big differences between the Bible writers and us, and will help you read and understand them better.

3. The Bible and Tradition – Catholic Christians have sacred Tradition in helping to understand the Bible. In fact, sacred Tradition and the Bible go hand in hand in communicating God's revelation to us. The church believes it continues to be empowered by the Holy Spirit to preserve, teach and interpret the Bible in every new generation.

On a practical level, this means there are plenty of resources to help us with any questions we have about the Bible, including Catholic books and websites, and parish priests and teachers. We shouldn't be afraid to use the rich resources the church has to offer us.

Handle with care

If you believe that the Bible came from God – however you think that happened – then you should approach reading it with care. God is on the other end of the line, and God is hugely unknown, mysterious, creative and wild. You simply do not know what might happen if you start reading with an open mind and expectant heart.

Here's some good advice from a 7th-century Christian, Isaac of Nineveh, about what to do before opening this wonderful book...

Never approach the words of the mysteries that are in the scriptures without praying and asking for God's help. Say, "Lord, grant me to feel the power that is in them." Reckon prayer to be the key that opens the true meaning of the Scriptures.
– Isaac of Nineveh

Around the Bible in 30 days

This short reading course is designed to help you **get started** in the Bible. Or if you're stuck, to help you get restarted. It introduces **30 significant** Bible passages that will take you quickly from Genesis to Revelation. Just think. If you read one a day, it'll take you a month. Unless it's February.

☐ 1. 'Let there be light!'
Genesis 1:1 – 2:4
The Bible opens with a majestic description of God as creator of everything. Humankind is seen as the peak of God's creation.

☐ 2. The Garden of Eden
Genesis 2:5 – 3:24
This second creation account focuses on Adam and Eve. Chapter 3 describes 'The Fall', when God's good creation is spoiled.

☐ 3. God tests Abraham
Genesis 22:1–9
Abraham (see page 56) was the father of the Jewish race. Here God tests his loyalty severely.

☐ 4. The burning bush
Exodus 2–3
Centuries after Abraham, the Israelites are slaves in Egypt. Moses (see page 62) is here called by God to help free the slaves.

☐ 5. The great escape
Exodus 14
The Israelites slaves have been set free. But they are pursued by the Egyptians and trapped against the sea (see page 61).

☐ 6. At Mt Sinai
Exodus 19:1 – 20:21
Moses' people reach Mt Sinai in the desert. Here God makes an agreement with them and gives them his law.

☐ 7. 'Be holy...'
Leviticus 19
In this chapter of laws, God wants his people to reflect his character. The laws have a special concern for the poor and powerless.

□ 8. David meets Goliath

1 Samuel 17

Over 200 years after Moses, the nation of Israel is under threat from its enemies, the Philistines.

□ 9. Elijah calls down fire

1 Kings 18

100 years after David's death, Israel is again under threat – this time from the worship of false gods such as Baal (see page 90).

□ 10. Elisha and Naaman

2 Kings 5

Elisha was successor to Elijah (see page 91). In this episode, God's concern and care for non-Jews comes across.

□ 11. God the Shepherd

Psalm 23

The best-known of all the psalms. This picture of God as a shepherd was echoed by Jesus in John chapter 10.

□ 12. David's repentance

Psalm 51

2 Samuel 11:1 – 12:23 is the historical background to this psalm. David desperately seeks God's forgiveness.

□ 13. Wise sayings

Proverbs 23

A chapter full of straightforward advice about practical living. This chapter is typical of the book of Proverbs.

□ 14. Isaiah called by God

Isaiah 6

Isaiah (see pages 122-23) sees God, has his sins forgiven, and is sent as a prophet to Israel.

□ 15. 'Comfort my people'

Isaiah 40

These words were written to encourage the Jews in exile (see page 92). It gives a vivid picture of the all-powerful God.

□ 16. The suffering servant

Isaiah 52:13 – 53:12

Over 500 years before Jesus suffered and died, Isaiah prophesied about God's servant who suffered for others.

□ 17. Valley of dry bones

Ezekiel 37:1–14

Ezekiel's strange vision is partly about the revival of Israel as a nation after the exile (see page 128).

□ 18. Daniel in the lions' den

Daniel 6

In the exile, Daniel reached a powerful position in the Babylonian royal court (see pages 132-33). Here his faith is tested.

□ 19. Sermon on the mount

Matthew 5–7

Some of Jesus' most famous teaching. Here he talks about how his followers should live out the new life of God's kingdom.

□ 20. Jesus the healer

Mark 5

In three stories, Jesus' power over evil, disease and death is dramatically seen in action.

□ 21. Jesus is crucified

Mark 14–15

The plots of Jesus' enemies finally reach a climax. But his death is no accident. It is part of God's plan and it is what Jesus came for.

□ 22. "He is risen!"

Luke 24

These stories are at the heart of the Christian faith. Jesus appears to his followers as the destroyer of death.

☐ 23. The ascension

Acts 1:1–11

Forty days after he is raised from death, Jesus ascends to heaven to share in his Father's glory.

☐ 24. The day of Pentecost

Acts 2

Seven weeks after Jesus' resurrection, the first Christians are filled with the power of the Holy Spirit (see page 207).

☐ 25. On the road to Damascus

Acts 9:1–31

Paul, violent persecutor of Christians, is dramatically converted on the road to Damascus (see pages 212-13).

☐ 26. The storm at sea

Acts 27

Paul is on his way to Rome, where he faces trial before the emperor. This storm shows how he acted under pressure.

☐ 27. Love

1 Corinthians 13

Paul wrote this letter to a church torn apart by pride. This famous passage shows what their first priority should be.

☐ 28. Christian living

Ephesians 5–6

The writer tells one of the first churches how Christians should live in the midst of a hostile world.

29. Christ, firstborn Son

☐ *Colossians 1:15–23*

This passage spells out the true identity of Jesus Christ. As head of God's new creation, he reconciles people to God.

☐ 30. New heaven, new earth

Revelation 21–22

The Bible closes with the final defeat of evil and the re-creation of heaven and earth by the King of kings and Lord of lords.

Intro to the Old Testament

Our reading is from the first book of Eliphazzzzz

If you make a list of the Bible's 10 longest books, they all come from the Old Testament (see the page opposite for the run-down). The Old Testament is a lot heftier than the New Testament, and it has a high count of books which look hard to read.

Because of this, it's a closed book for a lot of people. They might dip into the Psalms occasionally, or glance at the prophets, or know some of the famous stories like David and Goliath, but generally they don't really know what to do with it. All that history, all those battles, all those lists of families and tribes – is it really worth reading it?

Some Christians have suggested getting rid of the Old Testament entirely and having just the New.

The trouble is, if we don't read the Old Testament, then we miss out on a lot. Sticking to the New Testament and ignoring the Old is like walking into a movie when the film is two-thirds of the way through.

OK, you're going to see the dramatic ending and you're going to find out what happened in the end – but think of what you're missing. You're missing the car chase, the love scene, how it all started, some of the funniest scenes, some of the most tragic moments, and worst of all, you won't understand quite a lot of what you see because you've missed so much of the story.

In other words, the Old and the New Testaments are part of a single story. In reading the Bible, it's important to be there from the first reel. This doesn't have to mean reading from Genesis to Revelation in strict book order. But it's important to read the Old Testament so that we can see the New in its true colors.

As well as giving us the beginning of the story, the Old Testament also has qualities the New doesn't have – for example, timescale. The New Testament was written over a very short space of time – in just 80 or 90 years the whole thing was finished. The New Testament is a dynamic book, written against the clock. And its subject is a crisis in the story of God and the human race – the coming of Jesus. That's why it has great power and urgency – enviable qualities in any book.

But with the Old Testament, you've got time on your side. About 1,000 years of time, in fact. That's how long they had to write it. And so the Old Testament can afford to go at a slower pace. It can reflect on the everyday reality of life and how God relates to us as human beings in the here and now.

For example, the Old Testament tells stories, issues instructions and gives lots of space to...

- the family
- honesty and fair dealing in business
- experiencing depression
- showing justice to the poor and oppressed
- being a good friend
- facing anger or failure

There are a lot of different dimensions here – moral, political, emotional, legal, sexual, social, personal, commercial... the Old Testament reflects all these different facets of life in a way the New Testament can't. That's not downgrading the New Testament. It has its particular strengths, just as the Old Testament does. They are doing different jobs and they complement each other

The biggest books

Here's the top 10 of the biggest books in the Bible, with their word counts in brackets (43.7k = 43,700 words approx.)...

1. *Psalms (43.7k)*
2. *Jeremiah (42.7k)*
3. *Ezekiel (39.4k)*
4. *Genesis (38.2k)*
5. *Isaiah (37.0k)*
6. *Numbers (32.9k)*
7. *Exodus (32.6k)*
8. *Sirach (28.7k)*
9. *Deuteronomy (28.5k)*
10. *2 Chronicles (26.0k)*

to give us the full movie. Jesus, who was raised on the Old Testament and loved its teaching, said...

> **Every teacher of the Law who has been instructed about the kingdom of heaven is like the owner of a house who brings out of his storeroom new treasures as well as old.**

Matthew 13:52

New treasure and old treasure: the owner of the house brings them both out because they are equally a delight to him. That's how it is with us. This old treasure in the first part of the Bible has so much to give us. It is as much God's word to us as the New Testament.

Christians traditionally divide the Old Testament into four sections, based on the order of books in the Christian Bible (see page 11)...

- Pentateuch (Genesis to Deuteronomy)
- Historical Books (Joshua to 2 Maccabees)
- Poetry & Wisdom (Job to Sirach)
- Prophets (Isaiah to Malachi)

All the books are written in Hebrew and Greek apart from Daniel, which is partly in Aramaic. In the next few pages, we're going to explore these four sections of the Old Testament.

The Pentateuch

The first five books of the Old Testament open with what must be the most famous words to start any book: "In the beginning, God created the heavens and the earth..."

The alternative Old Testament

The Christian scheme of dividing the Old Testament into four sections of law, history, poetry and prophets isn't the only way to divide it up. In the Hebrew Bible, the books are ordered and grouped differently, in three sections...

Genesis
Exodus
Leviticus
Numbers
Deuteronomy

The Law (Torah) is the heart of the Hebrew Bible. These five books give the community God's commandments, which are like a blueprint for living as God's chosen people.

Joshua
Judges
1 & 2 Samuel
1 & 2 Kings
Isaiah
Jeremiah
Ezekiel
Hosea
Joel
Amos
Obadiah
Jonah
Micah
Nahum
Habakkuk
Zephaniah
Haggai
Zechariah
Malachi

Psalms
Proverbs
Job
Song of Songs
Ruth
Lamentations
Ecclesiastes
Esther
Daniel
Ezra
Nehemiah
1 & 2 Chronicles

The Prophets (Neviim) include all the books of the prophets found in the Christian Old Testament, plus six of the "history" books: Joshua and Judges, plus 1 and 2 Samuel and 1 and 2 Kings. This looks strange, but the reasoning behind it is shrewd: the history books are not straightforward factual accounts of what happened, but seek to explain the meaning of it all. They are prophetic in trying to show God's purpose behind events.

The Writings (Ketuvim) are all the books left over from the Law and the Prophets, and they were probably accepted into the Hebrew Bible last of all.

For an introduction to this section of the Old Testament, see page 52.

These books – known in the Hebrew scriptures as "the Torah", which means "the Law", are at the heart of Judaism, and they are at the heart of the Old Testament as well. So we need to understand them.

Now you might say, "I've never read a legal textbook in my life, and I'm not about to start doing it now!" If so, here's some good news. Even though these books are called "the Law", only two of them (Leviticus and Deuteronomy) are filled with lists of laws. The other three are nothing like a legal textbook.

Imagine opening a modern law book and finding inside not just rules and regulations, but stories – really exciting, almost racy stories – plus bits of poetry and a few songs. Can you imagine a judge breaking into song in court? And yet this is exactly the sort of material you'll find in these books. Genesis, Exodus and Numbers are built on storytelling. You can find out how to follow the story, and how to find the legal sections, on page 53.

If you're new to the Bible, or if you haven't read a lot of the Old Testament, the books to watch here are Genesis and Exodus. It's a good idea to read these two books because they're especially important. You can read Exodus straight after Genesis, as it continues the story.

The first 11 chapters of Genesis are among the strangest chapters of the Bible and their picture of God seems quite dark and primitive. In them, we find stories which are still widely known and talked about in our culture...

- Adam and Eve and the Garden of Eden
- Cain and Abel and the first murder
- Methuselah, at 969 the world's oldest man
- Noah and the flood
- The Tower of Babel and the origin of different languages

These ancient stories of beginnings and how things went wrong grab the imagination, and they tell us a lot about God and what he expects of the human race. And all the time, people grow in numbers and spread across the earth. It looks as if the only command of God they took seriously was: "go forth and multiply"!

And then we reach Genesis 12, and the story of Abraham and Sarah, the father and mother of the Israelites. And it's here that the whole story of the Old Testament gets going. It starts with an adventure story. Abraham is its unlikely hero. He's 75 years old (you'd think all his adventures would be behind him instead of in front of him!), he's living a quiet, comfortable life in the middle-eastern city of Haran, he's well respected, he's settling down into old age – when something happens to spoil it all. God speaks to him...

> **Leave your country, your relatives, and your father's home, and go to a land that I am going to show you. I will give you many descendants, and they will become a great nation.**

Genesis 12:1–2

So what does Abraham do with this strange request? He does what the disciples of Jesus did, when he met them on the seashore and said, "Follow me". He didn't know where he was going or what adventures he would have. Instead, he went into the unknown on God's say-so. That is faith.

And so the Bible takes to the road. Abraham packs up his household, gathers together his flocks, herds, servants, camels, animal-minders, his family and the tents they are to live in, says

The Bible: Hieroglyphic Version

goodbye to family, friends and neighbours, and the whole lot of them set out on the 800 miles to Canaan.

The rest of Genesis is taken up with the story of Abraham and Sarah's family. These are fantastic chapters to read, because this family is no collection of plaster saints. These are intensely human people, with big faults and big strengths.

The next key figure after Abraham is Jacob, the secondhand car salesman of the Old Testament. Honest Jacob: "I'm not here to cheat you, I'm here to treat you."

He swindles his brother, runs away to save his life, falls in love with his cousin (gorgeous, pouting Rachel), is tricked by her father into marrying her (less gorgeous, less pouting) older sister Leah, and ends up having 12 boys and a girl by his two wives and two concubines. The Old Testament's like that. And along the way there's a great deal of humor, tragedy and some startling encounters with God.

It is this that makes these stories truly great. We read them not because they're racy or amusing or tragic or larger than life – although they're all these – but because they show us God.

There's nowhere else in the Old Testament that we get such encounters with God as we find in Genesis and Exodus. Abraham, Jacob and Moses have a relationship with God that we don't find again until we come to Jesus himself. Here we have people arguing with God, wrestling with God, haggling with God, trying to get the best deal from God; people who struggle and will not let go of God – and a God who in turn will not let go of them.

Jacob and two of his wives: for a family tree of Abraham's family, see page 57.

On with the story. One of Jacob's twelve sons is Joseph, famous for his multicolored coat – and also close to God. His story starts in Genesis 37. He's sold into slavery by his brothers, but despite

THE BIBLE FROM SCRATCH

this bad career move Joseph becomes a big name in Egypt. By the end of the book of Genesis, the whole extended family – aunts, uncles, hordes of children, and even Grandad Jacob himself – go to live in Egypt as an honored family.

The book of Exodus picks up the story where Genesis leaves off. The time is a few generations after Joseph, and there's been a dramatic fall from grace for the Israelites. (Jacob's alternative name was "Israel", which is why his descendants started to be called the "Israelites".)

Suddenly, Egypt is under new management. And Jacob's family, which has been doing rather nicely, is chucked on the scrapheap. They become slaves on the world's biggest building site – forced to construct some of the buildings which put Egypt on the holiday brochures. Read about it in Exodus chapter 1. Where now is the God of Abraham, Isaac and Jacob? How are they going to become the "great nation" as promised by God to Abraham?

It's at this crucial point in the story that the key figure of the Old Testament arrives on the scene – Moses. He tells the despairing Israelite slaves that he has met the God of their fathers in the unlikely form of a burning, talking bush out in the desert. He tells them that the Lord has heard their cries of despair, and has sent him, Moses, to set them free.

The Israelite leaders believe him, but the ordinary people aren't convinced. When Moses speaks to Pharaoh, demanding he let the slaves go free, and Pharaoh responds by doubling their workload, the slaves are even less convinced by Moses and his God.

The trouble was that the average Israelite, even though he belonged to Abraham's family, didn't believe that the Lord was the only God. He was just one of many gods. And in Egypt, the

Joseph's life was punctuated by strange dreams. See page 59 for an outline of his life.

other gods were in charge – powerful gods like Ra, the sun god; Osiris, the god of vegetation; Anubis, the god of the dead. How could the God of Abraham possibly deliver them from Egypt? It wasn't his territory.

What happens next is astonishing – and the people of ancient Israel were never to forget it. In Exodus chapters 7–10, the Lord terrorizes Egypt with 10 great plagues, designed to convince Pharaoh to let the Israelites go free and to show his total power over any pretend gods. As locusts descend, the Nile turns to blood and the animals die, as the sun is blotted out in thick darkness – it seems as if all the ancient gods of Egypt are each dealt a humiliating knockout blow.

Finally, Pharaoh is forced to relent before the last terror – death itself. In Exodus chapter 12, an angel of death goes through the country at night, killing the firstborn sons of Egypt, but he passes over the Hebrews' homes which are daubed with the blood of a sacrificed lamb. This event is still remembered every year in Judaism at the festival of Passover. It also points us forwards to Jesus himself, who was sacrificed at Passover time.

The Israelites are free, and after saying a final (and terminal) farewell to the troops of Pharaoh on the borders of Egypt, they reach Mt Sinai, where they set up camp. Moses goes up the mountain and an agreement (or covenant, or testament) is forged between God and the new nation: they promise to live as his people, and he in turn promises to be their God.

Part of this agreement is the famous Ten Commandments of Exodus chapter 20, which act as a sort of summary of the whole of the Law of Moses. You can read that Law in all its detail in the books of Leviticus and Deuteronomy.

THE BIBLE FROM SCRATCH

These events – the Passover, the escape from Egypt, the giving of the Law – are the foundations of the Old Testament. The later books of the Bible frequently look back on these events and reflect on them, or build on them. The prophets say, "Remember what God did for you, how he freed you from slavery."

When the people of the Old Testament looked back on the exodus, they saw it as Christians see the death and resurrection of Jesus. They thought of Moses as their founding figure – just as Christians see Jesus as theirs. He was that important to them.

The history books

The Old Testament was lived and written in one of the most argued-about regions of the world. The land of Canaan is the meeting point of three great continents, connecting Europe, Africa and Asia. In ancient times all the great trade and war routes passed through this narrow strip of land.

This little corridor between the desert and the deep blue sea was always busy with important traffic. Armies often marched through it on their way to war – or they stayed and turned the land itself into a battleground.

At different periods of its history, the superpowers of the time turned their attention to ancient Israel – Egypt, Babylon, Assyria, Persia – and, later still, the Greeks and the Romans. The country's strategic position partly explains why there is so much violence in the history books of the Old Testament.

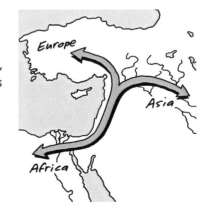

The history books are arranged mostly in chronological order. Joshua and Judges, the first two of them, pick up the story after the death of Moses. When people say that the Old Testament is full of battles and bloodshed, these are the books they are chiefly talking about. It could be said that this material should

For an introduction to the history section of the Old Testament, see page 72.

carry a health warning of some kind, because most of it makes depressing reading, and some of it can make you boil with rage.

After Moses died, Joshua became his successor. He led the people into Canaan, the land they believed had been promised to Abraham by God centuries earlier. The trouble was, Canaan belonged to other people, who had made their home in the country themselves. The result was the warfare described in the book of Joshua.

During this terrible struggle, Joshua managed to establish a foothold in the country. This is often described as "the conquest" of Canaan. But in fact, the invasion was far from successful.

What followed was 150 years of guerilla warfare, as ancient Israel's enemies, inside and outside the country, fought back. The story of that 150 years is told in the book of Judges, perhaps the wildest and grimmest of all the Old Testament books. It shows how the Israelites and their enemies lurched from crisis to crisis, killing and being killed, living in confusion and fear.

But there was something more than military action going on. This was as much a battle for the hearts and minds of the Israelites as a battle for territory, because the people were turning to other gods. They were probably still a long way from believing that their God was the only God. It's likely that they saw him as a local god with local powers. They believed that the Lord was powerful out in the desert, where he'd defeated the Egyptians and given them the Law – but how powerful was he in Canaan?

And there was another question. God might be good at winning battles, they thought, but what about farming? Surely the god Baal and his lover Anat were the experts you turned to when you wanted to make sure your crops would grow? Maybe this kind of questioning made the ordinary people drift over to the cruel gods of Canaan, who demanded child sacrifice and ritual prostitution.

They were desperate times. The Israelites had no overall leader. But what they did have was a series of colourful, 'wild west' characters who were able to rally the troops and lead them against their enemies. These local heroes were called the judges – but they ruled by the sword, rather than by the law.

The book of Judges is dominated by twelve of these wild, powerful (and often lawless) figures. There was Gideon, who defeated the massed armies of Midian with a clever trick and just 300 men. There was Samson, who couldn't keep his hair – or his pants – on. And there was the greatest of them all – Deborah, the only female judge. Deborah's cunning battle plan against the cruel King Jabin is still admired by military experts today. You can read about her in Judges chapters 4 and 5.

In the end, the wild and unpredictable leadership of the judges gave way to ancient Israel's first kings. The handover took place during the time of Samuel, who some claim as the last of the judges, and others as the first of the prophets. You can read about Samuel in 1 Samuel.

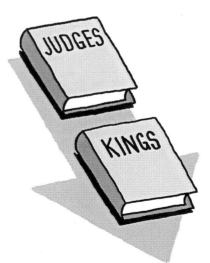

Samuel was against the whole idea of kingship, but his was a minority voice. The people were for it and they told Samuel what they wanted...

> **We want a king, so that we will be like other nations, with our own king to rule us and to lead us out to war and to fight our battles...**
>
> *1 Samuel 8:19–20*

If the Israelites thought they were solving all their problems by switching their system of leadership from judges to kings, they had a sharp shock coming. First onto the throne was Saul. He failed to defeat the country's enemies and ended up a broken man who got out by killing himself.

Then there was David, who was so close to God as a young man that even God was a fan, calling him "a man after my own heart". But once he became king, he also became corrupt. He went to bed with Bathsheba, the wife of one of his soldiers, and then arranged for her husband to be "accidentally" killed in battle. He was a hopeless father, and his weak family leadership led to the death of two of his sons and plunged the whole kingdom into civil war. His last words were to his son Solomon: "Make sure you kill all the people who did me harm." Heart-warming, eh?

The tragic story of David gives us one of the most wonderful story sequences in the Old Testament. If you want to read a section of the Bible that comes very close to a novel, full of drama and psychological insight, then read 2 Samuel chapters 11–19, which take you from David and Bathsheba right through to the unexpected death of... whoops, almost gave away the ending.

After David came Solomon, who is still a popular symbol for fabulous wisdom and even more fabulous wealth. But Solomon too was ruined by kingship. In those days, prestige points were awarded not for the size of your income, or the make of chariot you drove, but for the number of wives you could support. Solomon had 700. And in case of emergency, he also had 300 concubines on standby.

Solomon's indulgent lifestyle pulled him away from God. He began to worship other gods and he oppressed his people, turning some of them into slaves.

And after Solomon's time? Solomon's son Rehoboam came to the throne with a manifesto that was hardly a vote-winner...

> **My father made your yoke heavy; I will make it even heavier. My father scourged you with whips; I will scourge you with scorpions.**
>
> *1 Kings 12:14*

The result was civil war between north and south, and the kingdom split in two. The northern kingdom was known as Israel, and the southern kingdom was called Judah. From then on, there's a long downhill slide in the history books, with a dreary procession of kings that ends in despair, with first Israel and then Judah being conquered by Assyria and Babylon, the superpowers of their day.

During this long decline, the kings and other leaders were criticized and attacked by the prophets – men who saw visions, heard God speaking to them, and preached "the word of the Lord". Look ahead to page 45 for more on the prophets.

In the year 588 BC, the mighty Babylonian army arrived outside the walls of Jerusalem. After an 18-month siege, the wall of the city was smashed open. The last thing the King of Judah saw were his sons being put to death, and then he was blinded. He and his people were chained and force-marched 800 miles into exile. The Temple of the Lord was set on fire and the city turned into a ruin. You can read about this in 2 Kings 25.

These horrific events broke the faith of many of God's people. We're not just talking about a city being destroyed (though that's

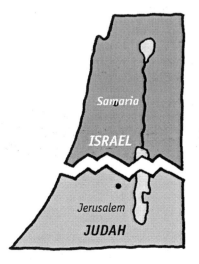

Samaria

ISRAEL

Jerusalem

JUDAH

bad enough) or a building called the Temple being burned to the ground. This city was God's city, and the Temple was the sign of his presence – and that presence was now gone. It seemed that the gods of Babylon had destroyed the God of ancient Israel, and there was nothing left to hope for or believe in. This was not just the destruction of a nation, but the destruction of a faith.

The Israelites were back in slavery – just as they had been in Egypt, all those centuries earlier.

Ezekiel, one of the prophets living in exile in Babylon, brought the people messages from God in those desperate times. In the despair of exile, and the despair of knowing that Jerusalem was destroyed, he began to preach hope. Ezekiel told his fellow exiles that God would do the impossible: he would bring them home.

And that is exactly what did happen. Around 60 years after the first exiles arrived in Babylon, they were allowed to return home to make a new start. Eventually, the Jewish people rebuilt the temple and the walls around Jerusalem.

After Alexander the Great conquered Palestine in 332 BC, the Jews were again under foreign domination. In 166 BC they won back their independence under the leadership of Judas Maccabeus and his family. This freedom lasted until 63 BC, when the Romans conquered the region. The Romans were still in control when Jesus was born.

You can read about the return from exile in the books of Ezra and Nehemiah.

EXILE

Poetry and wisdom

The Old Testament has poetry and songs scattered throughout its pages. There are songs that celebrate a victory, mourn a death, or tell a story. These songs were probably the earliest bits of the Old Testament to be told – they were treasured and passed on by word of mouth from generation to generation.

For an introduction to this section of the Old Testament, see page 106.

The songs celebrated events and told important stories for the children and adults of ancient Israel, putting into music what God had done for them in the past. Here are some of these early songs of the Old Testament...

■ **The songs of Moses and Miriam** – celebrating the escape from Egypt, and the drowning of Pharaoh's army (Exodus 15).

■ **The song of Deborah and Barak** – this song celebrates another victory in battle for the Israelites, and in fact the song gives us more details about the battle than the story which surrounds it (Judges 5).

■ **David's lament** – King Saul has been killed in battle, alongside his son Jonathan, and David laments their death. Saul had been the sworn enemy of David, but Jonathan had been his closest friend...

Saul and Jonathan —
in life they were loved and gracious,
and in death they were not parted.
They were swifter than eagles,
they were stronger than lions.
How are the mighty fallen
in the midst of the battle.
2 Samuel 1:23, 27

David is probably the most talented person in the Bible: he's famous for being a king, a psalm-writer and a harpist... not to mention his giant-slaying skills. For more on David, see pages 84 and 112.

■ **The song of the vineyard** – a number of the prophets wrote their messages as poetry. This song is one of the best examples, giving us a devastating picture of Israel's broken-down faith (Isaiah 5:1–7).

While there's poetry and song throughout the Old Testament, and especially in the books of the prophets, all the books in the poetry and wisdom section are written either completely or partly as poetry. The book of Psalms is the most famous of these books, and was the songbook of ancient Israel, as well as later being the songbook of many branches of the church. The psalms reflect a wide range of emotions – everything from joy, thankfulness and faith in God, through to anger, despair, doubt and revenge.

The Psalms contain pilgrims' songs, coronation anthems, songs of national triumph, prayers from the depths, wedding songs and more. Several of the psalms come complete with little instructions which tell the music director which tune to use in singing the psalm. These tunes have intriguing names, such as "the lily of the covenant", "the doe of the morning", "a dove on distant oaks", and most enigmatic of all, a tune called "do not destroy".

Sadly, all of these tunes, as far as we know, have been lost. However, we do know how some of the psalms were sung because several of them tell us. Psalm 150, for instance, says...

Praise him with the sounding of the trumpet,
praise him with the harp and lyre,
praise him with tambourine and dancing,
praise him with the strings and flute,
praise him with the clash of cymbals,
praise him with resounding cymbals.
Let everything that has breath praise the Lord.
Psalm 150:3–6

These noisier psalms must have been very lively and oriental, much like the sinuous music you can still hear today in the Middle East.

What is the value of the Psalms for us? Basil the Great, writing in the 4th century AD, had this to say...

The book of Psalms heals the old wounds of the soul and gives relief to recent ones. It cures the illnesses and preserves the health of the soul. Every psalm brings peace, soothes the internal conflicts, calms the rough waves of evil thoughts, dissolves anger, corrects and moderates profligacy. Every Psalm preserves friendship and reconciles those who are separated. Who could actually regard as an enemy the person beside whom they have raised a song to the one God?
- Basil the Great

Also famous is the little book called the Song of Songs, a title that literally means "the best of all songs". This is one of the most beautiful books of the whole Bible, and it's a love poem, a poem of sexual love. It takes us back to God's creation of man and woman in Genesis chapter 1, when God looked at these sexual beings and said, "It is good". And so this poem uses a fabulous wealth of oriental imagery to celebrate human love.

The poetry in the Psalms and the Song of Songs bursts with brightly colored images and rich, extravagant language. In these poems, trees clap their hands; hills sing for joy; God's enemies melt like wax; the sun is so eager to rise that he's like a bridegroom going to his wedding; the beloved's teeth are like a flock of sheep; God rides on the clouds; and his Law is sweeter than honey, dripping from the comb.

These powerful – and at times childlike – images have great riches to offer us. As we see these human emotions laid bare, we can learn so much about our inner selves, our relationships, our God – and we can enjoy this extravagant language for its own sake.

Job, Proverbs, Ecclesiastes, Wisdom and Sirach draw on the Bible's Wisdom tradition (see page 107). Along with the Song of Songs, they had a rather rocky time making it into the Old Testament at all. Questions were asked about them. Are they too negative (Job and Ecclesiastes)? Doesn't it contain contradictions (Proverbs)? Isn't it too sexy (Song of Songs)?

We can be grateful that they were all finally included, because the Wisdom books ask some of the biggest and darkest questions of all – where is God when innocent people are suffering? Job puts his questions very sharply, asking, for example, "Is God evil?" And Ecclesiastes several times reaches the conclusion that life is ultimately meaningless.

Look at these words from Job. Job is speaking to God, and his words start off by sounding like a song of praise...

> **You have given me life and constant love, and your care has kept me alive...**

... but then they suddenly turn into a terrible accusation...

> **... but now I know that all the time you were secretly planning to harm me.**

Job 10:12–13

THE BIBLE FROM SCRATCH

This is a terrible thought about God: that he appears to be good, but is actually preparing the next horror. And yet this might be a familiar thought to anyone who has suffered terribly.

It's important that these thoughts are recorded in the Bible. If the decision about which books were allowed in and which were to be thrown out was being made today, then probably those who hold the Bible in highest regard would reject these "questionable" books. And then verses such as the ones in Job would be censored out – and we'd be left with a "nice" faith, rather than a faith which addresses our darkest fears about God.

The Bible doesn't hold back from asking the toughest questions. In a world where two-thirds of the people are hungry, we need to ask these questions. Our faith is strong enough to take them.

The prophets

The final section of the Old Testament contains the books of the prophets. Their position at the end of the book doesn't mean they were added as an afterthought – quite the opposite. Jesus often referred to the Old Testament scriptures as "the Law and the Prophets", which shows how important the prophets are.

For an introduction to this section of the Old Testament, see page 120.

But who were the prophets? And what did they do? One way of thinking about them is as the authentic leaders of the people, as chosen by God.

In the Old Testament, the Israelites experienced two very different types of leadership which we can call dynamic leadership and dynastic leadership. This is how they worked...

- First, there was a strong tradition of **dynamic leadership**. These were people who had been specifically chosen by God and were specially gifted by him for the task of leadership.

Here's the contract...

- But later on, the people demanded **dynastic leadership** – they wanted a dynasty. They wanted leaders who were leaders not because God had specially called or gifted them, but because their father had been leader before them.

For example, how did Moses become leader? God called him in the desert, appearing in the sign of a burning bush which did not burn up. How did Samuel become leader? As a child, he slept next to the ark of the covenant, and one night he was awoken by a voice calling him by name. The voice was God's.

Moses and Samuel were raised up as dynamic leaders. So too were the judges, although their form of leadership was rather low-grade when compared to Moses, who was later reckoned to be the greatest of all the prophets.

But the people grew tired of this style of leadership. They had no control over it. They couldn't wait around all the time for God to chose a leader! They wanted a smooth, trouble-free succession from ruler to ruler. The sort of leadership you could set your watch by – not unpredictable and full of surprises as God is. They wanted a dynasty.

And that is what they got. We can see the switchover in 1 Kings chapter 1, where David boldly makes the change while he's lying on his deathbed. He says...

Solomon will succeed me as king, because he is the one I have chosen to be ruler of Israel and Judah.

And a court official responds...

> **May the Lord your God confirm it.**

1 Kings 1:35–36

In other words, God was being quietly demoted. His role was simply to rubber-stamp David's choice. David had betrayed the tradition that had made him king in the first place, because like Moses and Samuel he had been raised up from nowhere. And so it happened that after David died, there was a scramble for power and Solomon had his rival butchered. That was how leadership in ancient Israel was to be decided from now on.

However, the tradition of dynamic leadership carried on. It simply worked outside the new, violent tradition of kingly rulers. It was as if God had abandoned the kings and switched to Plan B. His influence would now be felt not through the official leaders, chosen by the establishment, but through his own agents, chosen in the same dynamic way he had chosen Moses, Deborah, Gideon and the others. These subversive agents of God were the prophets.

The first of them actually appear in the history books of the Old Testament. There are extensive stories about the two main prophets during the early era of the kings: Elijah and Elisha (see pages 87 and 91). But the later prophets such as Isaiah and Jeremiah don't appear in the history books. Instead they have their own books in the prophecy section at the end of the Old Testament, even though a number of them lived during the time of 1 and 2 Kings. If that sounds rather complex, it's because it is.

How did the prophets work, and what did they achieve? Here are four ways of looking at them.

Unpopular prophets

Here's a rundown of the Bible's most persecuted prophets...

*1. **John the Baptist** – beheaded in prison for criticizing King Herod's marriage.*
*2. **Jeremiah** – thrown into a cistern for predicting the fall of Jerusalem.*
*3. **Elijah** – fled into the desert when Queen Jezebel tried to have him killed.*
*4. **Daniel** – left overnight in the King of Babylon's den of lions for insisting on praying to the Lord.*
*5. **Ezekiel** – ridiculed for his strange prophecies.*
*6. **Jonah** – swallowed alive by a big fish... although it was Jonah's own fault this happened.*

1. They spoke to their own generation – the prophets frequently filled the well-known role of "prophet of doom" in their preaching. They thundered when the people worshipped other gods, denounced rich employers for cheating their workers, attacked kings for making disastrous alliances with other nations and raged against Israel as a whole for failing to follow the Law of God. They also looked into the future and warned about what would happen if their hearers ignored what they were saying.

The prophets were obstinate and difficult and took no hostages. They were frequently unpopular and risked their lives for the messages they preached. Here's the prophet Elijah on a bad day, complaining to God about the cost of being a prophet...

> I have been very zealous for the Lord God Almighty. The Israelites have rejected your covenant, broken down your altars, and put your prophets to death with the sword. I am the only one left, and now they are trying to kill me too.

1 Kings 19:14

2. They took the people back to Moses – the prophets based their message on the Law of Moses and the covenant God made with the Israelites on Mt Sinai. They did this because they saw the event on Mt Sinai as the defining moment of the Israelites' relationship with God – so much so that several prophets pictured the relationship as a marriage. The problem was that Israel was having an affair with other gods – she was betraying the marriage. Their response was moral outrage.

3. They transformed the faith of ancient Israel – the prophets did more than simply remind the people of what Moses had said.

They also received revelations from God which expanded the faith they had received. A great example of this can be seen in the way Isaiah celebrates God as Lord of the universe, while ridiculing all other "gods" as mere inventions...

> **Do you not know? Have you not heard? The Lord is the everlasting God, the Creator of the ends of the earth. He will not grow tired or weary, and his understanding no one can fathom.**

Isaiah 40:28

Many biblical experts believe the impact made by the prophets caused the Law of Moses to be written down for the first time. If this is true, then the prophets ensured that the Law was passed on, as well as basing their message on it.

4. They looked ahead to the future – the prophets are famous for pointing beyond their times to the coming age of the messiah. Christians believe their prophecies were fulfilled in the birth, death and resurrection of Jesus, and in the descent of the Spirit on the Day of Pentecost.

Matthew's Gospel in the New Testament follows up what the prophets had to say about the future messiah by matching specific messages to specific incidents in the life of Jesus (see page 176). If we look at the wider picture, though, we can see that the prophets were longing for the time to come when God would decisively act in human history and make it possible for people to know him for themselves.

The prophet Joel seems to be leaning forward out of the Old Testament and into the New when he says...

I will pour out my Spirit on all people.
Your sons and daughters will prophesy,
your old men will dream dreams,
your young men will see visions.
Even on my servants, both men and women,
I will pour out my Spirit in those days.
Joel 2:28-29

MOSES

The Bible opens with five books that are known as the **Pentateuch**, or the **Law of Moses** (or in Hebrew, the **Torah**). Pentateuch means "five-part writing". These books set the agenda for the whole Bible and they're referred to again and again throughout the Old and New Testaments. Here's a quick rundown of them all...

Genesis – the beginning of the universe, the human race and the family of Abraham

Exodus – how the Israelites were freed from slavery in Egypt in the time of Moses, their greatest-ever leader

Leviticus – a manual of laws to help the Israelites live together in peace and justice, and to worship God

Numbers – the Israelites' wilderness years, wandering in the desert under the leadership of Moses

Deuteronomy – Moses' greatest hits... the speeches he gave before the people occupied the land of Canaan

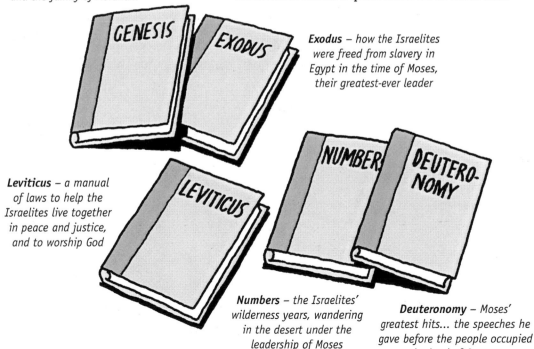

INTRO

The Bible starts with five books of _laws_? Not a great start, is it? Why didn't they put them at the back?

The **five books of the Law** are right up at the front because they're so important to the rest of the Old Testament. The Law was a whole **way of life** and it was at the heart of ancient Israel's relationship with God. The rest of the Bible refers to the Law many, many times.

Hmm. Well... if it's all the same with you, I'll speed on to where the action starts.

If you do that you'll miss some of the **best stories** in the Bible. These books aren't just full of rules and regulations. They have family quarrels, songs, battle accounts, larger-than-life characters and the famous stories of the creation and the exodus.

Why are they called 'the Law'?

All five books were once believed to have been **written by Moses**. The central event of the books is when God gives Moses the Law on **Mt Sinai**. The books are often simply called 'the Law of Moses'.

The book of Genesis is a fairly easy read as it's **full of action.** But Exodus, Leviticus, Numbers and Deuteronomy are harder work, because the storyline is mixed in with **blocks of laws.** Here's how to sort it out...

FINDING THE LAWS

Exodus 20:1–17 – the Ten Commandments, given to Moses by God on Mt Sinai

Exodus 21–23 – called 'The book of the covenant', it gives lots of different laws

Leviticus – a manual of social and religious laws (see page 66)

Deuteronomy – this word means 'the second Law' – at the end of Moses' life, Moses reminds the people of the Law (see page 69)

FOLLOWING THE STORY

Exodus 1–19 – out of Egypt

Exodus 20–24 – God gives Moses the Law on Mt Sinai

Exodus 32–34 – the people worship a golden calf

Exodus 40 – the tent for worship is set up

Numbers 10–14 – they leave Sinai and moan at Moses

Numbers 16–17 – rebellion breaks out

Numbers 20–24 – they have success near the promised land

Deuteronomy 31 and 34 – the death of Moses

LOVING IT

For the Israelites, the Law was **the very heart** of the Old Testament. These quotes show how much they valued the Law...

Psalm 19

The law of the Lord is perfect. It gives new strength.

If someone studies the law, they come to know the will of God.

A Jewish rabbi

How I love your law! I think about it all day long!

Psalm 119

Genesis is a Greek word that means **origins**. We get "generate", "genes" and "genealogy" from the same root word. It's a **book of beginnings**, as its famous opening words say: "In the beginning, God created the heavens and the earth..." The book traces origins in **two ways**...

- The origin of the **universe** and the **human race** (Genesis 1–11)
- The origin of the **people of God** (Genesis 12–50)

Genesis chapters 1–11 include some world-famous stories...

The Creation (Genesis 1):
God creates heaven and earth in six days

The Garden of Eden (Genesis 2–3)
Adam and Eve sin and are driven out

The first murder (Genesis 4)
Cain slays his brother Abel

The great flood (Genesis 6–9)
Noah's floating zoo preserves life from the flood

The tower of Babel (Genesis 11)
The great tower falls, leading to confusion

54

CREATION

The creation story in Genesis 1... what do people make of it?

Christians believe different things about it. Here are three of the majority viewpoints...

Days = 24-hour days – God creating everything in six days is an exact description of how it all happened. Most Christians in the pre-scientific era believed this. Today it is the view of "creationists".

Days = eras – Each "day" of the creation story represents a period of time – possibly millions of years. The creation account shows the order of creation. This theory was developed in the 19th century in response to scientific discoveries.

Days = artistic – The Genesis 1 account has a beautiful structure and is close to being poetry. The author wasn't interested in chronology but wanted to reflect artistically on why God created the universe. The origins of this view go back to St Augustine (4th–5th century AD).

Just another creation myth?

Experts argue over how much the creation in Genesis is similar to the myths of ancient Babylon.

Here are some **similarities** in the Babylon myths...

- the first human is created from clay
- a female is called 'the lady of the rib'
- a crafty serpent lives in a tree

And here are some **differences**...

- there's no actual moment of creation
- the world is made from the body of a murdered god
- the gods are constantly quarrelling

None of the ancient myths have the great qualities of Genesis 1, with its **one God**, distinct from his creation, and with God declaring that all he has made is **good**.

ABRAHAM

Abraham? Who he?

> Big-bearded chap, wasn't he?

Abraham gets **star billing** in the Bible – he's up there with Moses, Elijah and all the other bearded wonders. Jewish people still think of him and Sarah as their ultimate **father and mother**. They lived around 1900 BC.

Read Abe and Sarah's story in Genesis 12–25

The big thing about Abraham is **his faith in God.** He was living quite happily in a town called Haran when God told him to go to a faraway country he'd never seen because God wanted to give it to him.

And even though Abraham and Sarah were seriously old, God told them they were going to have a child and give birth to **a whole nation...**

> er... just the one baby will be fine, thanks...

Look up at the heavens and count the stars... So shall your offspring be.

God explains the deal in Genesis 15:5

Ancient Soap

Abraham and Sarah's children and grandchildren grew into a clan that eventually became the **Israelites**. The story of those first generations (Genesis 12–50) is quite soap opera-ish. The family tree opposite explains some of the relationships.

ABE & SARAH'S FAMILY TREE ▶

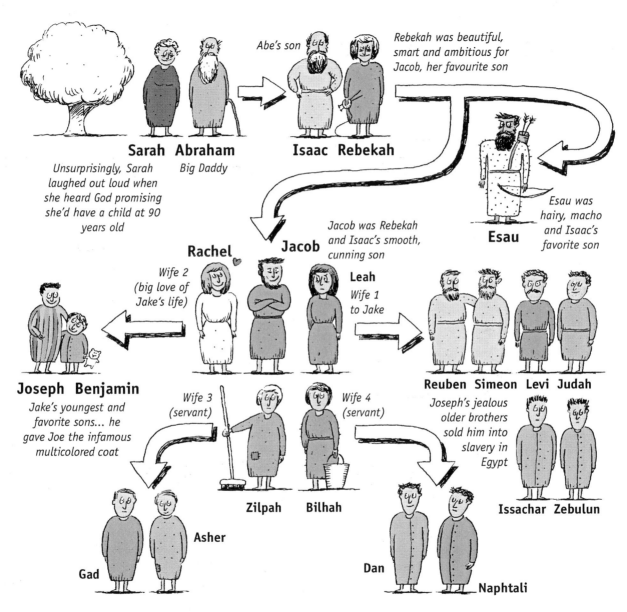

Sarah **Abraham**

Big Daddy

Unsurprisingly, Sarah laughed out loud when she heard God promising she'd have a child at 90 years old

Abe's son

Isaac **Rebekah**

Rebekah was beautiful, smart and ambitious for Jacob, her favourite son

Esau

Esau was hairy, macho and Isaac's favorite son

Rachel

Wife 2 (big love of Jake's life)

Jacob

Jacob was Rebekah and Isaac's smooth, cunning son

Leah

Wife 1 to Jake

Joseph **Benjamin**

Jake's youngest and favorite sons... he gave Joe the infamous multicolored coat

Reuben **Simeon** **Levi** **Judah**

Joseph's jealous older brothers sold him into slavery in Egypt

Wife 3 (servant)

Zilpah **Bilhah**

Wife 4 (servant)

Issachar **Zebulun**

Gad **Asher**

Dan **Naphtali**

Abraham & Sarah's Travels

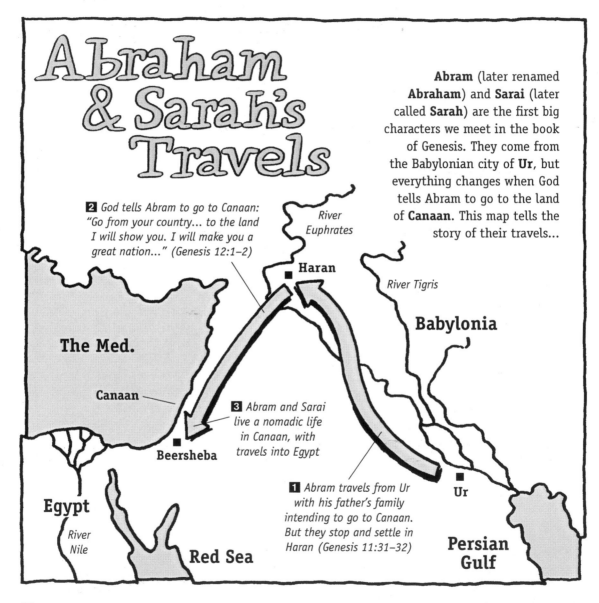

Abram (later renamed Abraham) and Sarai (later called Sarah) are the first big characters we meet in the book of Genesis. They come from the Babylonian city of Ur, but everything changes when God tells Abram to go to the land of Canaan. This map tells the story of their travels...

2 God tells Abram to go to Canaan: "Go from your country... to the land I will show you. I will make you a great nation..." (Genesis 12:1–2)

River Euphrates

River Tigris

Haran

Babylonia

The Med.

Canaan

3 Abram and Sarai live a nomadic life in Canaan, with travels into Egypt

Beersheba

1 Abram travels from Ur with his father's family intending to go to Canaan. But they stop and settle in Haran (Genesis 11:31–32)

Ur

Egypt

River Nile

Red Sea

Persian Gulf

JOSEPH

Joseph's story in the book of Genesis is one of the most gripping and surprising in the Bible. This chart gives an idea of the ups and downs of his career. Read the story yourself in **Genesis 37** and **39–50**. It has a surprise ending (which we're not going to give away, naturally)...

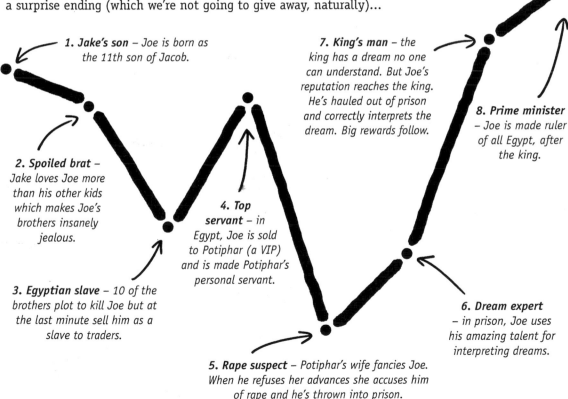

1. Jake's son – Joe is born as the 11th son of Jacob.

2. Spoiled brat – Jake loves Joe more than his other kids which makes Joe's brothers insanely jealous.

3. Egyptian slave – 10 of the brothers plot to kill Joe but at the last minute sell him as a slave to traders.

4. Top servant – in Egypt, Joe is sold to Potiphar (a VIP) and is made Potiphar's personal servant.

5. Rape suspect – Potiphar's wife fancies Joe. When he refuses her advances she accuses him of rape and he's thrown into prison.

6. Dream expert – in prison, Joe uses his amazing talent for interpreting dreams.

7. King's man – the king has a dream no one can understand. But Joe's reputation reaches the king. He's hauled out of prison and correctly interprets the dream. Big rewards follow.

8. Prime minister – Joe is made ruler of all Egypt, after the king.

EXODUS

Exodus (like the word "exit") means "going out". The book has this title because it tells the greatest story of Israel's history – when Abraham's descendants **escaped from slavery** in Egypt.

The book of Exodus divides into **two parts**...

1 The great escape

Exodus 1–18 – Over 400 years after the time of Joseph, the Israelites are slaves in Egypt. But God hears their cries for help and calls **Moses** to lead them to freedom. The Egyptians don't want to release them, and even after they have escaped, try to recapture them.

2 The great agreement

Exodus 19–40 – Moses leads the people into the desert. They reach **Mt Sinai**, which Moses climbs to meet God. Here God makes a **covenant** (or "agreement") with his people. He gives them...

- Moral, social and religious laws to live by.
- Instructions on making the tent and ark which will be the focus of Israel's worship.

RED SEA

SINAI DESERT

EGYPT

In part one, they travel from Egypt to beyond the Red Sea...

... in part two, they travel through to Mt Sinai

MT SINAI

THE GREAT ESCAPE

How they got out of Egypt

1. MOSES vs. PHARAOH

God gives Moses a **fearsomely difficult** job to do: releasing the Israelites from their 400-year-old slavery in Egypt.

To help Moses persuade Pharaoh it's a good idea to let his slaves go, God gives Moses **amazing powers**, such as turning his stick into a snake – and back again. But Pharaoh's not impressed.

So God sends a series of **plagues** on Egypt: blood, frogs, gnats, flies, animal disease, boils, hail, locusts and darkness (Exodus 7–10).

I was a perfectly decent walking stick 'til I met Moses...

2. THE PASSOVER

Despite the plagues, Pharaoh still wants to keep his slaves, so God tells Moses to get ready for Plan B... the **Passover**.

At midnight, God will kill all the **firstborn sons** in Egypt. The Israelites are to eat a special meal, with lamb. The lamb's blood is to be painted on their doorposts outside, and when the angel of God sees the blood, he'll "pass over" the house, sparing the Israelite sons.

After this terrible night, in which **Pharaoh's own son dies**, the Israelites are told to go.

Let my people go!

Moses in Exodus 5:1

3. CROSSING THE RED SEA

Then Pharaoh has a change of heart and sends his army to **recapture** the Israelites. The army traps them at the Red Sea (see map on page 64).

But there is one last surprise up the divine sleeve. In Exodus 14 God uses a strong wind to make a way through the sea. The Israelites **escape**, while the Egyptians are **drowned**.

MOSES

Moses is the main man in four whole books! He must have been quite a hero to get this kind of billing.

Yes... no one in the Old Testament is given as much space as Moses. **His birth** is at the beginning of Exodus, and **his death** is at the end of Deuteronomy, and in between, he's the **starring character**.

Despite the top billing, Moses had an **unpromising start**. His people were living under brutal conditions as **slaves** of the Egyptians. As a young man, he was wanted for **murder** and he became a **fugitive**. He fled into the desert, where he lived for many years.

The turning point in Moses' life was his **encounter with God** in the desert, when he saw a bush on fire which didn't burn up. From out of the burning bush, God called him...

Moses, Moses!

God told Moses to lead his people **out of slavery** in Egypt. Moses asked for the name of the God who was asking him to do this, and God famously replied...

I am who I am.

Read Moses' encounter with God at the burning bush in Exodus 3–4.

Here's an outline of Moses' life →

What the? This isn't the pizza I ordered!

■ As a baby, Moses was rescued from the **River Nile** by an Egyptian princess (Exodus 2).

■ He **murdered an Egyptian** who was beating a Hebrew slave. A wanted man, he fled into exile (Exodus 2).

■ He **encountered God** in the desert and was called to lead the Israelites out of slavery (Exodus 3)...

■ He led his people to **freedom** (Exodus 5–12), crossing the sea safely while the Egyptians drowned.

■ At **Mt Sinai**, he received God's Law (Exodus 20).

■ Because he **failed God** at a critical moment, he wasn't allowed to enter the promised land, although he died in sight of it (Numbers 20).

■ **Moses died** and was buried by God (Deuteronomy 34).

Moses is a major figure in the Bible and in Judaism...

There never has been a prophet in Israel like Moses. The Lord spoke with him face to face.

Deuteronomy 34:10

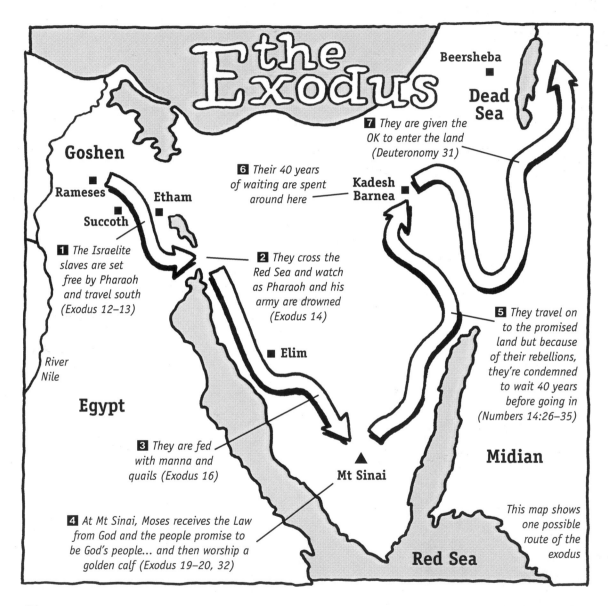

the Exodus

Beersheba

Dead Sea

Goshen

7 They are given the OK to enter the land (Deuteronomy 31)

Kadesh Barnea

6 Their 40 years of waiting are spent around here

Rameses

Etham

Succoth

1 The Israelite slaves are set free by Pharaoh and travel south (Exodus 12–13)

2 They cross the Red Sea and watch as Pharaoh and his army are drowned (Exodus 14)

5 They travel on to the promised land but because of their rebellions, they're condemned to wait 40 years before going in (Numbers 14:26–35)

River Nile

Egypt

■ **Elim**

3 They are fed with manna and quails (Exodus 16)

▲ **Mt Sinai**

Midian

4 At Mt Sinai, Moses receives the Law from God and the people promise to be God's people... and then worship a golden calf (Exodus 19–20, 32)

This map shows one possible route of the exodus

Red Sea

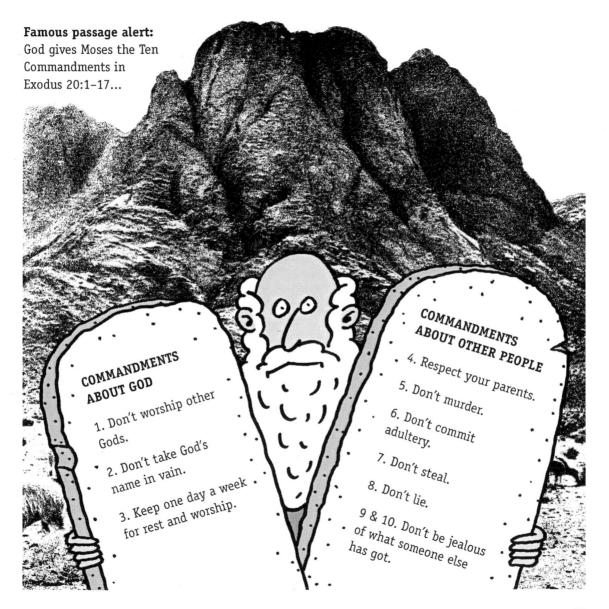

Famous passage alert:
God gives Moses the Ten
Commandments in
Exodus 20:1–17...

COMMANDMENTS ABOUT GOD

1. Don't worship other Gods.

2. Don't take God's name in vain.

3. Keep one day a week for rest and worship.

COMMANDMENTS ABOUT OTHER PEOPLE

4. Respect your parents.

5. Don't murder.

6. Don't commit adultery.

7. Don't steal.

8. Don't lie.

9 & 10. Don't be jealous of what someone else has got.

THE BIBLE FROM SCRATCH

LEVITICUS

Here's a key quote from this book...

I am the Lord your God, and you must keep yourselves holy, because I am holy. Leviticus 11:44

Some typical laws...

> Do not hold back the wages of a hired man overnight.
> *Leviticus 19:13*

> Do not abandon me and worship idols; do not make gods of metal and worship them.
> *Leviticus 19:4*

Leviticus 19:36

> Use honest scales and honest weights.

phew!

Leviticus 19:32

> Do not eat pigs. They must be considered unclean; they have divided hooves, but do not chew the cud.
> *Leviticus 11:7*

> Show respect for the elderly and revere your God.

Never one of the most popular bits of the Bible, Leviticus is still quite an amazing book. It lays down the law about how the community of ancient Israel should **live and worship**.

The laws cover treatment of slaves, paying fair wages, not marrying your sister, etc. Laws about **worship and sacrifice** rub shoulders with laws for **everyday living**, showing God's concern for the whole of life.

Leviticus in 5 mins! Read chapter 19, which gives the flavour of the whole book.

THE BIBLE FROM SCRATCH

NUMBERS

Welcome to book 4 of the 5 books of Moses. In the Hebrew scriptures this book is called **In the Wilderness**, but the Christian Bible always calls it Numbers, because in it Moses **counts all the people** while they are in the desert.

"In the Wilderness" is probably a better title, though, because the book is about the way the Israelites **rebelled** against God and were made to **wander** in the wilderness for 40 years.

The crisis of the book happens when God says...

> You will die here in this wilderness. Your children will wander in the wilderness for forty years, suffering for your unfaithfulness, until the last one of you dies.

Numbers 14:32–33

Nice. So how does the book work?

Like this...

■ The people **leave Mt Sinai** (Numbers 1–10).

■ They moan about **the food,** so God feeds them (Numbers 11).

■ **12 spies** are sent on a mission into the promised land. 10 of them bring back a bad report and the people refuse to

enter the land. God condemns them to wander in the desert for 40 years (Numbers 13–14).

■ **38 miserable years** follow (Numbers 15–19).

■ As the people approach the promised land, the **local kings** try to stop them (Numbers 20–24).

The Ark

The ark of the covenant is the most **mysterious object** of the Bible. "An army which carries the ark before it is invincible," claimed Indiana Jones in the movie *Raiders of the Lost Ark*. So how about it? What's the story of the ark?

The ark was made in the time of Moses. The **Ten Commandments***, written on two tablets of stone, were inside. It was about 4 feet long and covered with gold (Exodus 37).*

It was kept in an inner sanctuary where God met with Moses – it symbolized the **presence of God** *with his people.*

*What happened to the ark? Some think it **disappeared** when Jerusalem was sacked by the Babylonians. Others say it still exists and is in Ethiopia, or is buried somewhere in Israel/Palestine.*

An Egyptian chest carried by priests. The ark was probably modelled on a box like this.

*When the Israelites crossed the **River Jordan** into the promised land, priests carried the ark into the river and the waters parted, allowing the people across (Joshua 3).*

King David *wanted to bring the ark to Jerusalem. On the way, a man touched the ark to stop it falling off a cart and was **struck dead** (2 Samuel 6).*

*They suffered seven months of **disease** and eventually sent the ark back to Israel (1 Samuel 5–6).*

*The Israelites' big enemy, the **Philistines**, captured the ark in a battle (1 Samuel 4).*

DEUTERONOMY

Think of Deuteronomy as **Moses' Greatest Hits**. The book is a collection of **speeches** he gave just before the Israelites entered the **promised land**, after 40 years of going in circles in the desert. Here they are (numbers in brackets are chapters in Deuteronomy)...

Speech 1 – Moses recalls all God has done for his people and sums up: "The Lord is God in Heaven and Earth. There is no other God. Obey all his laws... and all will go well with you" (1–4).

Speech 2 – Moses preaches on the 10 commandments. The most famous words of the book are here: "Hear, O Israel! The Lord our God, the Lord is one. Love the Lord your God with all your heart..." Jesus called these words the greatest law of the Old Testament (5–26).

Speech 3 – Moses on the curses if the people disobey God, and the blessings if they obey (27–28).

Moses' Song – No sweet song this, but a series of savage warnings about the perils of abandoning God (32).

Speech 4 – Moses makes a big appeal for commitment to God. "Today I am giving you the choice between good and evil, between life and death" (29–30).

Moses' Blessing – Moses' final words are to bless each of the tribes of Israel – except Simeon, which was later absorbed into Judah (33).

Highlights

from the Pentateuch

The creation
Genesis 1:1 – 2:4
God creates heaven and earth in six days.

The Garden of Eden
Genesis 2:5 – 3:24
Adam and Eve, that snake and a tempting piece of fruit.

Noah's flood
Genesis 6:9 – 8:22
God drowns the world, but spares Noah and his family.

The tower of Babel
Genesis 11:1–9
Building a giant tower leads to an explosion of languages.

Abraham to sacrifice Isaac
Genesis 22:1–19
God puts Abraham to the ultimate test of loyalty.

Jacob cheats Esau
Genesis 27:1–45
Jacob steals the family birthright from his brother.

Jacob's ladder
Genesis 28:10–22
On the run, Jacob dreams that God is with him.

Moses and the burning bush
Exodus 3
Moses encounters God in the desert and his life is changed.

Crossing the Red Sea
Exodus 14:10–31
The Israelites escape slavery by crossing the sea on dry land.

The 10 Commandments
Exodus 20:1–17
God reveals his Law to Moses on Mt Sinai.

HISTORICAL BOOKS

Judges – troubled times as Canaan's original inhabitants strike back

Joshua – the Israelites invade the land of Canaan

This section of the Bible **tells the story** of the Israelites from just after the time of **Moses** until **134 years** before the time of Christ. There are 16 books, which look like this...

Ruth – the story of two women from the time of Judges

1 Samuel – King Saul rules as Israel's first king

2 Samuel – the reign of King David

1 Kings – King Solomon and the division of the kingdom into Israel and Judah

2 Kings – Israel and Judah fall and the people are taken into exile

1 & 2 Chronicles – the story of David and the other kings, but told in a different way

Tobit – An angel sorts out Tobit's family problems

1 & 2 Maccabees – Persecution of Jews and their resistance during the time of Greek rule

Ezra – the exiles return to Jerusalem

Nehemiah – the ruined walls of Jerusalem are rebuilt

Judith – Judith boldly delivers her people from a Babylonian invasion

Esther – Queen Esther saves the Jewish people from a holocaust

INTRO

If you looked up these 16 books in a Hebrew Bible, you'd find most of them in a big group of books called **the Prophets**. That group includes most of our "history" books, plus Isaiah, Jeremiah and all the other books of the prophets.

Sounds a bit strange...

Yes, it does... because when you look at them, they're not full of prophecies or predictions of the future. Instead, they tell the **story of the Israelites** from the time of Joshua (Moses' successor) to the time of the Maccabees – that's about 1100 years.

But they're classed as prophetic books because they're not just about the bare facts of the story. What the writers want to know is **how God is at work** in events, and what the unfolding story all means. And that makes them **prophetic** – because the job of prophets in the Old Testament is to relate God's message to what is happening.

Here's just one example of how these books act prophetically, interpreting the meaning of events...

Again the Israelites did evil in the eyes of the Lord, and for seven years he gave them into the hands of the Midianites...

Judges 6:1

stories

These books are brilliant at storytelling. For a quick taster, try these...

1 The **walls of Jericho** collapse Joshua 2 and 6

2 **Gideon** defeats Israel's enemies Judges 6–7

3 **David vs. Goliath** 1 Samuel 17

4 David and **Bathsheba** 2 Samuel 11–12

5 **Solomon prays** for wisdom 1 Kings 3

6 **Elijah** defeats the priests of the false god, Baal 1 Kings 18–19

7 **Elisha** heals Naaman in the Jordan 2 Kings 5

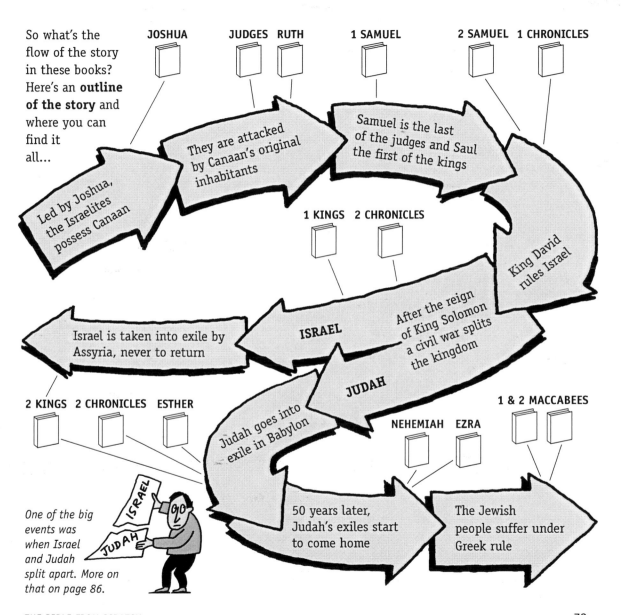

So what's the flow of the story in these books? Here's an **outline of the story** and where you can find it all...

JOSHUA

JUDGES RUTH

1 SAMUEL

2 SAMUEL 1 CHRONICLES

Led by Joshua, the Israelites possess Canaan

They are attacked by Canaan's original inhabitants

Samuel is the last of the judges and Saul the first of the kings

King David rules Israel

1 KINGS 2 CHRONICLES

After the reign of King Solomon a civil war splits the kingdom

ISRAEL

Israel is taken into exile by Assyria, never to return

JUDAH

2 KINGS 2 CHRONICLES ESTHER

Judah goes into exile in Babylon

NEHEMIAH EZRA

1 & 2 MACCABEES

50 years later, Judah's exiles start to come home

The Jewish people suffer under Greek rule

One of the big events was when Israel and Judah split apart. More on that on page 86.

THE BIBLE FROM SCRATCH

73

JOSHUA

The book of Joshua is an account of how the Israelites **attacked and occupied** the land of Canaan. The driving belief of the book is that God had **promised** the land to the Israelites as far back as the time of Abraham (see Genesis 15:18–21).

And?

The trouble was that the land of Canaan already **belonged to other people**, which makes Joshua a very bloody book. The occupation was only partly successful, and this caused the Israelites **big problems** in the time of the Judges.

Joshua is the main character in the book. He had been Moses' **right-hand man** since the time of the exodus from Egypt. He was a ruthless soldier and also an inspiring religious leader in the style of Moses.

A three-step campaign

According to the book of Joshua, the land was occupied in three stages...

1 Crossing the Jordan
They defeat the cities of Jericho and Ai (Joshua 1–8)

2 Southern campaign
Joshua wipes out five local southern kings (Joshua 9–10)

3 Northern campaign
A large army of Israel's enemies gather in the north, but a surprise attack gives Joshua victory (Joshua 11)

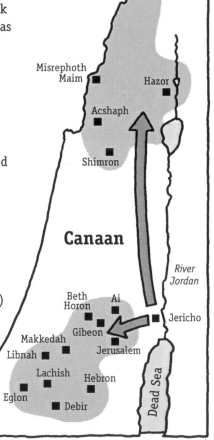

Misrephoth Maim

Hazor

Acshaph

Shimron

Canaan

River Jordan

Beth Horon

Ai

Jericho

Gibeon

Makkedah

Libnah

Jerusalem

Lachish

Hebron

Eglon

Debir

Dead Sea

Judges

Is this the bit where we come in?

Nope. Despite the name of the book, this isn't about judges as we know them today. The judges were **popular leaders** who became famous in the 150 troubled years after the time of Joshua. The Israelites had no settled system of leadership in those days and each of the judges came to rescue them during a **time of crisis**.

Judges is rather a heavy book. Its recurring theme is how the Israelites repeatedly **rebelled** against God and set in motion a grim cycle of events...

In the good times they forget God and worship the false gods of Canaan.

The good times return!

↖ *Start here*

This makes God unhappy.

God raises up a judge who rescues the Israelites from their enemies.

God allows the enemies of Israel to attack, defeat and oppress them.

See the next two pages for a complete list of judges, plus biogs of two of the most famous: **Deborah** and **Samson**.

Despair!

They cry out: "O Lord, please save us!", etc.

DEBORAH

Deborah is the **only female military leader** of the Old Testament. She became a national hero in Israel when the people were suffering under the violent rule of **King Jabin**, an invader from the north.

Deborah roused the nation to action. At her command, a military leader, **Barak**, gathered 10,000 men to fight King Jabin.

What made Jabin such an unbeatable enemy was his high-tech army, with its **900 iron chariots**. Undeterred, Deborah called her troops to the top of Mt Tabor, and Jabin hastened to the scene.

The Israelites charged down the mountain and drove Jabin's chariots into the marshes of the **River Kishon**, where they were useless. Jabin's army fled. See Judges 4–5 for the whole story.

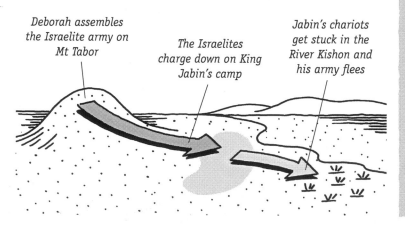

Deborah assembles the Israelite army on Mt Tabor

The Israelites charge down on King Jabin's camp

Jabin's chariots get stuck in the River Kishon and his army flees

Who were the judges?

Othniel – Judges 3:7–11
Ehud – Judges 3:12–30
Shamgar – Judges 3:31
Deborah (with **Barak**) – Judges 4–5
Gideon – Judges 6–8
Tola – Judges 10:1–2
Jair – Judges 10:3–5
Jephthah – Judges 10:6 – 12:7
Ibzan – Judges 12:8–10
Elon – Judges 12:11–12
Abdon – Judges 12:13–15
Samson – Judges 13–16

> The towns of Israel stood abandoned, Deborah. They stood empty until you came like a mother for Israel.

*Song of Deborah
Judges 5:7*

SAMSON

Samson was **the last** of the judges, and he was like someone out of the wild west – gritty, go-it-alone, trigger-happy and **supernaturally strong**. He's also famous for his dangerous relationship with gorgeous, pouting **Delilah**. Find him in Judges 13–16.

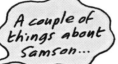

A couple of things about Samson...

1 During Samson's life, Israel was occupied by its old enemies, **the Philistines**. Although Samson never rallied an army to drive them out, he waged a one-man war against the Philistines.

2 Samson was raised as a **Nazirite**. This meant he made promises to be dedicated to God in a special way. He promised not to drink **alcohol**, go near a **dead body** or **cut his hair**. Samson broke all these promises in his life, and this led to his downfall.

Samson was larger than life. Alongside his trick of tearing down city gates bare-handed, he was also **a comic**. After killing some Philistines with a donkey's jawbone, he sang…

With an ass's jaw I heaped them on the floor!

This dark mixture of **slaughter** and **comedy** sums up Samson's wayward life.

Despite his many faults, Samson makes it into the list of heroes of faith in Hebrews 11:32. Early church writers saw his killing of a lion (see Judges 14:5–6) as a picture of Christ's defeat of Satan.

RUTH

A story from the time of Judges...

Ruth is a **short story** – it would take up seven pages in a paperback novel. Here's how it starts...

Elimelech and **Naomi** take their family from their home in Bethlehem to live in **Moab** (a foreign country). Then Elimelech dies. Naomi's two sons marry two **local girls**, one of them being Ruth.

But ten years later, the two sons die as well, and Naomi decides to go back home to Bethlehem. Ruth insists on **going back with her**, even though she will be a foreigner in Israel. Her loyalty to Naomi is impressive. She says...

A FAMILY HALVED

Elimelech   Naomi

Mahlon   **Ruth**   Orpah   Chilion

> Wherever you go, I will go, and your God will be my God.
>
> *Ruth 1:16*

The rest of the book of Ruth (from chapter 2) tells the story of how Ruth meets and marries **Boaz** (a relative of Naomi). The story is full of oriental details and is a good read.

Foreigners

Ruth is an example of non-Jews who were blessed by God. Naaman (in 2 Kings 5) is another example. God's love was not confined to one nation or race, even then.

12 TRIBES

The nation of Israel was made up of 12 families, each descended from one of the **sons of Jacob** (see page 57). These 12 families became the 12 tribes of Israel. These tribes are in the spotlight in the Bible several times...

1 When the nation entered the promised land, each tribe was given its own **piece of territory** to settle (Joshua 13–21) – see the map.

2 In the time of the judges, there was often **friction** between the tribes. Some were lazier than others when it was time to unite and fight a common enemy (Judges 5:13–18).

3 This friction was one reason why the ten northern tribes and the two southern ones split after the reign of King Solomon (1 Kings 11–12). From then on, the north was called **Israel**, and the south, **Judah**.

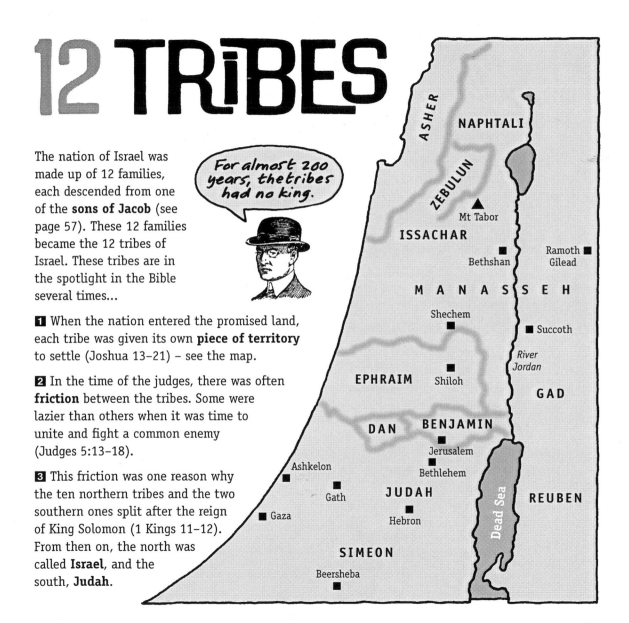

For almost 200 years, the tribes had no king.

ASHER
NAPHTALI
ZEBULUN
Mt Tabor
ISSACHAR
Bethshan
Ramoth Gilead
MANASSEH
Shechem
Succoth
River Jordan
GAD
EPHRAIM
Shiloh
DAN
BENJAMIN
Jerusalem
Bethlehem
Ashkelon
Gath
JUDAH
Dead Sea
REUBEN
Gaza
Hebron
SIMEON
Beersheba

1+2 Samuel

We'll take these two books in turn. First, 1 Samuel...

The book of 1 Samuel picks up where Judges left off. It follows the story of Israel as the nation moved from rule under the **judges** to rule under the **kings**...

Judges → Kings

Why did they want to **make the switch?**

Because the people of Israel were **sick of the Philistines**, their old enemies who pushed them around whenever they felt like it. They were also **sick of the judges**, whose leadership was unstable and unpredictable. They decided the answer was to have a king...

The **only person** who disagreed with it all was **Samuel**, the prophet at the time. He told the people that their kings would **tax them** into the ground and **treat them badly** – but it was no use.

Samuel was depressed about it, but God said: "You are not the one they have rejected. They have rejected me as their king" (1 Samuel 8:7).

We want a king!

Yeah! Like the other nations!

Someone to lead us in battle!

Someone who'll make us all rich!

Someone to go on the stamps!

tsk!

See 1 Samuel 8...

THE BIBLE FROM SCRATCH

Once it's decided they're going to have a king, 1 Samuel continues by telling the story of **King Saul**...

... while 2 Samuel tells the story of **King David**.

King Saul

The first king of Israel and regarded by everyone as a **complete flop**. Saul failed to defeat the Philistines once and for all, and he got on the wrong side of **Samuel**, who said that God had **rejected him** as king.

One of the big themes of 1 Samuel is Saul's **jealousy of David**. He once threw a spear at David during David's harp practice. Saul eventually committed **suicide**. Read his story in 1 Samuel 9–31.

temper!

King David

The second king of Israel and **best-known and loved** king of the Old Testament. His reign is seen as a **golden age** even though it had its dark moments. David is introduced in 1 Samuel 16 and his story continues right through 2 Samuel to end in 1 Kings 2.

David was **anointed secretly** by Samuel (in 1 Samuel 16) while Saul was still ruling. Once he became king, he was successful against his enemies, but a **disaster as a father**. His own son, **Absalom**, led a major revolt against him.

For a mini-biog of **Saul**, see page 83. And for one of **David**, see page 112.

Try reading 2 Samuel 9–20 and 1 Kings 1–2 in one go. It's one continuous story and is an amazing and dramatic read.

Samuel

Samuel is a controversial character. Is he the last of the **judges** (following on from Samson), or the first of the **prophets** (paving the way for **Elijah** and **Elisha**)? Was he just a local wise man whose reputation has been blown up out of all proportion, or the **national hero** he appears to be? The experts disagree.

Some Jewish biblical experts even used to think that Samuel was a **Nostradamus-like** character who wrote the whole of 1 and 2 Samuel, predicting in detail events which took place long after he was dead. He's always been argued over. Here are some of the **contradictions and confusions** of his life...

> Samuel opposed the people's call to have a king of Israel, but crowned both Saul and David.

> Samuel made Saul, but he also broke him. He chose Saul to become king, but later said God had rejected him. Saul never recovered.

> Samuel secretly anointed David king while Saul was on the throne. This led to incredible conflict.

One view is that Samuel was a meddler who undermined Saul and brought confusion and disaster on Saul and the people of Israel.

Samuel's life

Here are the key events in Samuel's life. The numbers in parentheses are chapters in 1 Samuel...

- Samuel is born (1)
- God calls young Sam (3)
- becomes leader (4)
- Samuel the ruler (7)
- Samuel and Saul (8-10)
- rejects Saul (15)
- anoints David king (16)
- Samuel dies (25)

KING SAUL

Saul is one of the most **tragic figures** in the Bible and one of the book's few suicides. Chosen as Israel's first king, he lost **the confidence** of Samuel and then lost **his mind.** Here's his career graph.

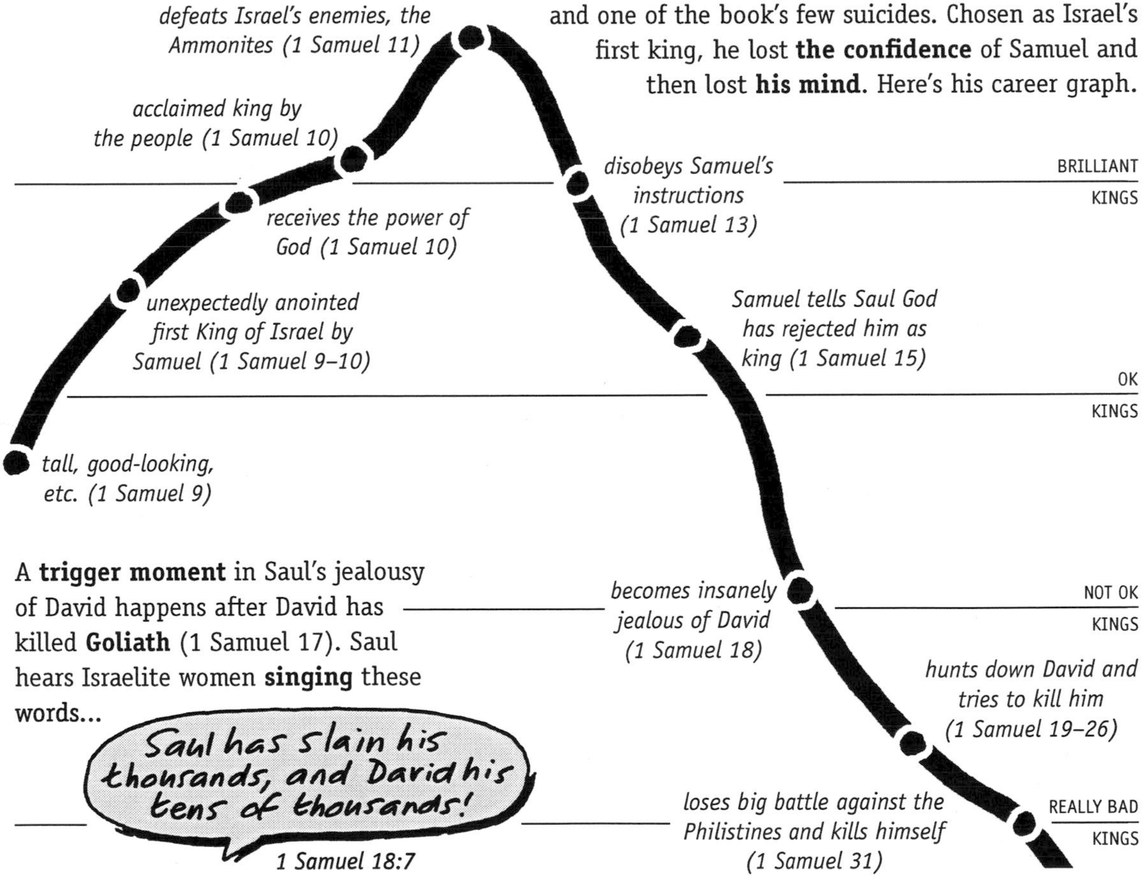

defeats Israel's enemies, the
Ammonites (1 Samuel 11)

acclaimed king by
the people (1 Samuel 10)

disobeys Samuel's
instructions
(1 Samuel 13)

receives the power of
God (1 Samuel 10)

BRILLIANT
KINGS

unexpectedly anointed
first King of Israel by
Samuel (1 Samuel 9–10)

Samuel tells Saul God
has rejected him as
king (1 Samuel 15)

OK
KINGS

tall, good-looking,
etc. (1 Samuel 9)

A **trigger moment** in Saul's jealousy of David happens after David has killed **Goliath** (1 Samuel 17). Saul hears Israelite women **singing** these words...

becomes insanely
jealous of David
(1 Samuel 18)

NOT OK
KINGS

hunts down David and
tries to kill him
(1 Samuel 19–26)

Saul has slain his thousands, and David his tens of thousands!

1 Samuel 18:7

loses big battle against the
Philistines and kills himself
(1 Samuel 31)

REALLY BAD
KINGS

DAVID'S SOAP

Enjoy **drama and intrigue**? The story of the royal family (David's) has them in plenty. Here's our guide to David's Soap Opera – David's **wives** are in the top row and his **kids** are below.

David had at least 10 wives and over 20 children. The children shown below are the major players.

David took Bathsheba to bed while she was married to someone else – and then had her husband killed (2 Samuel 11).

Ahinoam   Maacah   **David**   Haggith   **Bathsheba**

Amnon   **Absalom**   **Tamar**   **Adonijah**   **Solomon**

Amnon was attracted to his half-sister, Tamar. He lured her into a trap and raped her (2 Samuel 13). David was angry but did nothing.

Absalom had Amnon killed and fled from David's wrath. He led a rebellion against David but was himself killed in battle (2 Samuel 13–18).

Tamar became a recluse.

Adonijah tried to assume the throne when David was old. After David died, Solomon had him killed and became king himself (2 Kings 1–2).

SOLOMON

After David died, King Solomon won **the big prize** and became ruler of Israel. He had competition from one of David's other sons, but some behind-the-scenes **killing** did the trick. You can find Solomon's reign in the first eleven chapters of 1 Kings. He is still **famous** for three things...

WIVES

Today we measure wealth in houses, cars and bank balances. In Solomon's time you knew someone was rich if he could afford two or more wives. **Solomon had 700.** Plus 300 women in the royal harem.

WISDOM

At the start of his reign, Solomon **asked God for wisdom.** For the most famous example of his cleverness, see the story of the **two babies** in 1 Kings 3:16–28. Many of Solomon's wise sayings are said to be included in the book of **Proverbs.**

WEALTH

No doubt about it – Solomon was rich. He'd inherited a strong, secure kingdom from King David and he spent his life making it **fabulously wealthy.** Trouble was, he did it by oppressing his own people. He **taxed** them heavily and he used Israelites as **forced labor** on his building projects. This created anger which erupted after his reign.

1 KINGS

The book of 1 Kings covers a century of **big change** in Israel. First, King David dies. Then there's the reign of his son, **Solomon.** And after that the kingdom is **torn in two.** Like this...

SOLOMON'S KINGDOM

NORTHERN KINGDOM

SOUTHERN KINGDOM

ISRAEL – had an unstable monarchy. Kings were overthrown or assassinated to be replaced by other kings. Capital: **Samaria.**

JUDAH – was ruled in a more stable way by a succession of King David's descendants. Capital: **Jerusalem.**

1 Kings tells the story of this split (which was never healed). The book can be divided into three chunks:

1. The new king

1 Kings 1–2 records how Solomon became king after the death of his father, David.

2. Solomon's reign

1 Kings 3–11 is about the reign of King Solomon. It describes in detail the building of the **Temple in Jerusalem.** The Temple was to become the focus of worship for the Jewish faith. For more, see page 103.

3. The kingdom splits

Why did it happen?

The northern tribes of Israel resented Solomon's taxes and forced labour. When he died, they went into revolt.

And then?

The rest of 1 Kings tells the story of the different kings, north and south.

elijah

👑 **King Ahab** 👑

ROYALLY COMMANDS YOU TO
BE PRESENT AT HIS MARRIAGE
TO

Princess Jezebel

DAUGHTER OF KING ETHBAAL OF SIDON
AT
THE ROYAL CAPITAL —
SAMARIA

THE SERVICE WILL BE CONDUCTED
BEFORE THE GODS OF SIDON AND ISRAEL

BRING YOUR OWN GODS   RSVP

Elijah was a **powerful and extraordinary** prophet in the northern kingdom of Israel. His story runs from 1 Kings 17 to 2 Kings 2. Elijah has a big reputation in Judaism. Every year at Passover, a special **seat** and a **glass of wine** are set out for him.

Elijah lived during a dark period of Israel's history, 100 years after King David. **King Ahab** was on the throne and his marriage to **Jezebel** (a foreign princess who was positively evangelistic in her devotion to the god **Baal**) had shocked Israel. Jezebel was Elijah's deadly enemy.

Here are the **main episodes** from Elijah's life...

Drought – Baal is meant to be in charge of the weather and making crops grow. So Elijah announces that God is sending a three-year drought (1 Kings 17).

Competition – Elijah arranges a fire-starting contest between himself and 450 prophets of Baal. It's one of the most dramatic chapters of the Old Testament (1 Kings 18).

God's voice – Elijah has to run for his life from the fury of Jezebel. Alone and depressed, he encounters God on Mt Horeb (1 Kings 19).

Naboth – Ahab wants to make his garden bigger – but his neighbour, Naboth, won't sell his land – so Jezebel has him killed (1 Kings 21).

Exit – Elijah is taken up to heaven in a chariot of fire, watched by Elisha, his disciple and successor (2 Kings 2).

O Baal, answer us!

Shout louder! Surely he is a god! Maybe he is sleeping and must be woken up!

Elijah taunts the prophets of Baal in the contest on Mt Carmel (1 Kings 18)

KINGS OF ISRAEL

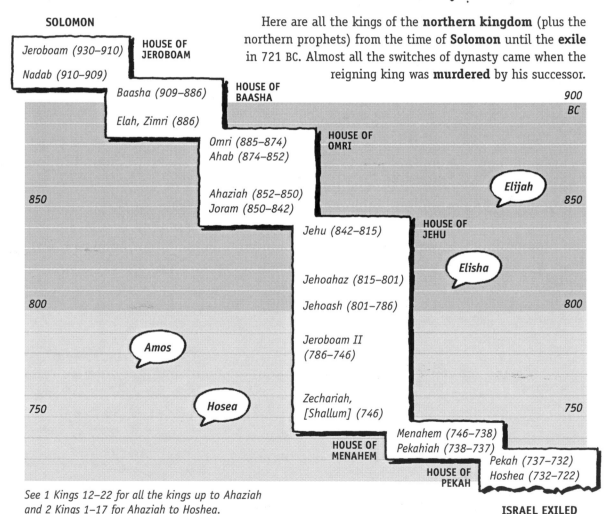

SOLOMON

Jeroboam (930–910)

Nadab (910–909)

HOUSE OF JEROBOAM

Baasha (909–886)

Elah, Zimri (886)

HOUSE OF BAASHA

Here are all the kings of the **northern kingdom** (plus the northern prophets) from the time of **Solomon** until the **exile** in 721 BC. Almost all the switches of dynasty came when the reigning king was **murdered** by his successor.

Omri (885–874)

Ahab (874–852)

HOUSE OF OMRI

900 BC

Ahaziah (852–850)

Joram (850–842)

Elijah

850

Jehu (842–815)

HOUSE OF JEHU

Elisha

Jehoahaz (815–801)

Jehoash (801–786)

800

Jeroboam II (786–746)

Amos

Zechariah, [Shallum] (746)

Hosea

750

Menahem (746–738)

Pekahiah (738–737)

HOUSE OF MENAHEM

Pekah (737–732)

Hoshea (732–722)

HOUSE OF PEKAH

See 1 Kings 12–22 for all the kings up to Ahaziah and 2 Kings 1–17 for Ahaziah to Hoshea.

ISRAEL EXILED

THE BIBLE FROM SCRATCH

KINGS OF JUDAH

In contrast to the northern kingdom of Israel, where kings were regularly **overthrown**, the kings of Judah right down to the last king, Zedekiah, were all **descended from David**.

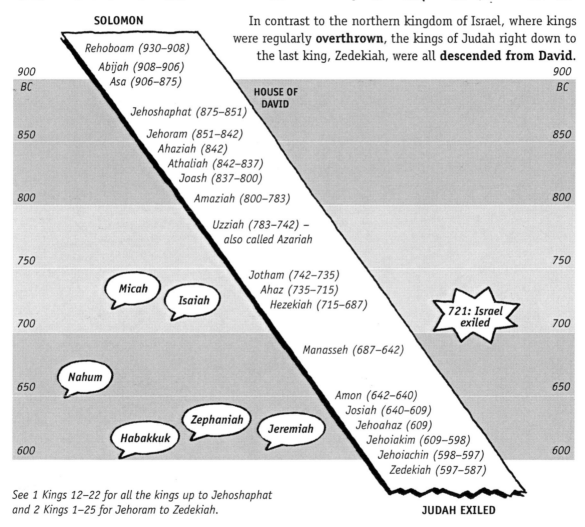

See 1 Kings 12–22 for all the kings up to Jehoshaphat and 2 Kings 1–25 for Jehoram to Zedekiah.

BAAL

Baal was the god **most actively worshipped** in Canaan, which is why his name comes up so regularly in the Old Testament.

Baal's area of expertise was **the weather**, which was pretty crucial. It was in Baal's power (so people believed) to **bless with rain** which made the crops grow and the land fertile. It was also in his power to **punish with drought** and famine, or with terrible floods. He was therefore a god to be feared and treated nicely.

So what threat was Baal to the Israelites?

They were **constantly tempted** to worship him as well as Yahweh (the name of the God of Israel). They hadn't yet got the idea that Yahweh was **the only God** and all other "gods" were human-made. They thought Yahweh was very powerful in the **desert**, where he had worked miracles in the time of Moses, but was he any good in **Canaan**? Could he make the crops grow?

The big showdown between Baal and God comes in a story about Elijah in 1 Kings 18. Baal fails to produce any rain after a three-year drought, while... well, read it yourself! It makes this ancient hymn to Baal sound a bit hollow...

Baal will make fertile with his rain... he will put his voice in the clouds, he will flash his lightning to the earth.

Baal was called the Thunderer, the Rider on the Clouds, the Prince of the Earth. He's shown here ready to strike with his spear-like thunderbolt. The image is from 1500-ish BC.

THE BIBLE FROM SCRATCH

2 KINGS

2 Kings **continues the story** of Israel and Judah from where 1 Kings left off. It charts the direction the two countries took as they headed on a collision course with disaster.

Within 150 years of each other, both nations had been taken violently **into exile** by the superpowers of the time. 2 Kings doesn't just tell us about these dramatic and shocking events – it also provides **an explanation** for why it all happened.

The real reason for the disaster, says 2 Kings, was that the kings of Israel and Judah led their people deeper and deeper **into sin**. Again and again the writer of 2 Kings tells us...

> He, like the kings before him, sinned against the Lord...

> Sins? What sins? Come on! Out with them!

They followed false gods and goddesses and compromised their faith in God

They sacrificed their children to the Canaanite gods

The rich oppressed the poor and kept them living in poverty

2 Kings 17:7–18 has a full list of reasons – and also see the book of Amos on page 128

Elisha

There are **very few heroes** in 2 Kings – but the prophet **Elisha** is one of them. He worked in Israel in the 50 years after Elijah. Elisha is famous for...

Witnessing Elijah's departure (2 Kings 2)

Providing oil for a starving family (2 Kings 4: 1–7)

Raising a dead boy back to life (2 Kings 4:8–37)

Healing Naaman, the commander of the Syrian army (2 Kings 5)

Predicting the sudden end of the siege of Samaria (2 Kings 6:24 – 7:20)

The Exile

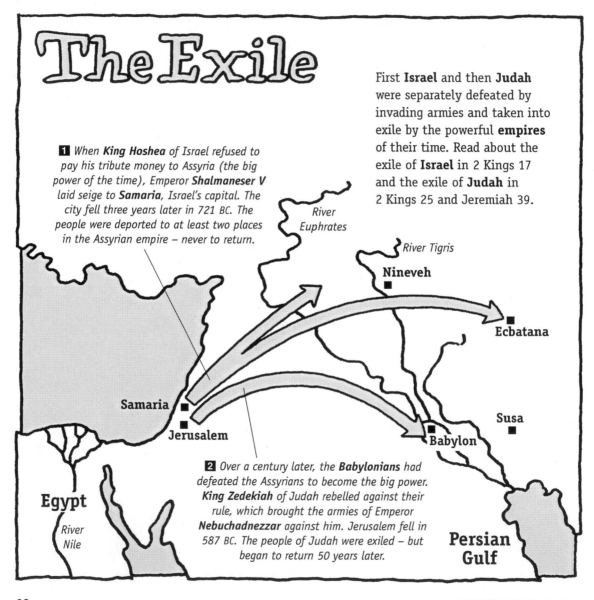

First **Israel** and then **Judah** were separately defeated by invading armies and taken into exile by the powerful **empires** of their time. Read about the exile of **Israel** in 2 Kings 17 and the exile of **Judah** in 2 Kings 25 and Jeremiah 39.

1 *When **King Hoshea** of Israel refused to pay his tribute money to Assyria (the big power of the time), Emperor **Shalmaneser V** laid seige to **Samaria**, Israel's capital. The city fell three years later in 721 BC. The people were deported to at least two places in the Assyrian empire – never to return.*

River Euphrates

River Tigris

Nineveh

Ecbatana

Samaria

Susa

Jerusalem

Babylon

2 *Over a century later, the **Babylonians** had defeated the Assyrians to become the big power. **King Zedekiah** of Judah rebelled against their rule, which brought the armies of Emperor **Nebuchadnezzar** against him. Jerusalem fell in 587 BC. The people of Judah were exiled – but began to return 50 years later.*

Egypt

River Nile

Persian Gulf

1 & 2 CHRONICLES

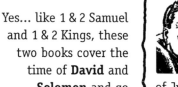

Hang on... this Chronicles book looks the same as Samuel and Kings...

Yes... like 1 & 2 Samuel and 1 & 2 Kings, these two books cover the time of **David** and **Solomon** and go through to the **exile of Judah** in Babylon. But 1 & 2 Chronicles tell the story in **a different way**.

So why did the writer tell it differently?

Well, the theory goes that these books were written for **the exiles** of Judah who started returning home from Babylon from the 530s BC. They needed to be **encouraged** that they were still part of David's kingdom, and that the temple and its worship were still important.

That's why **David** looks rather spotless in 1 & 2 Chronicles, and it explains the big emphasis on **the Temple**.

Different? Like how? Well, for example...

1 The books airbrush out **the scandalous bits** of David's life (e.g. his affair with Bathsheba), presenting him as a **hero** – and they pretty much ignore the **northern kingdom**.

2 Then they throw in a lot of material about **the Temple** and the religious side of Israel's life. Whoever wrote Chronicles **carefully selected** what he wanted to include.

The skeleton of the books

- Boring family trees (1 Chronicles 1–9)
- King Saul dies (1 Chronicles 10)
- King David's achievements (1 Chronicles 11–29)
- King Solomon's rule (2 Chronicles 1–9)
- The north-south split (2 Chronicles 10)
- Kings of Judah (2 Chronicles 11 – 36:12)
- Jerusalem falls to the Babylonians! (2 Chronicles 36:13–23)

EZRA

Chronicles, Ezra and Nehemiah make up a **four-volume set**. So if you've just read 1 and 2 Chronicles, Ezra **continues the story**.

So what's it all about?

The people of **Judah** were dragged off into exile in 587 BC and held captive in Babylon. But nearly 50 years later, Babylon was overthrown by **King Cyrus of Persia**. Cyrus was a more humane ruler, and he encouraged all Babylon's exiles to **return home**. Ezra describes what happened when some of the exiles got back to Jerusalem.

Ezra (who was a **priest**) is an important figure in the Bible's story. In exile, the Jewish people lost everything that held them together: their **king**, their **Temple** and **Jerusalem** itself. Ezra realized they'd have to start from scratch if they were going to survive. So he took them back to **the Law of Moses**.

Ezra helped his people find a new national focus in the law and in practices such as the **sabbath** and **circumcision**. This held the Jewish people together after the exile. They became known as **the people of the Book**.

Ezra makes a guest appearance in the book of Nehemiah (chapters 8–10) and does a reading of <u>all</u> the first five books of the Bible – that's almost 70 feet of scroll...

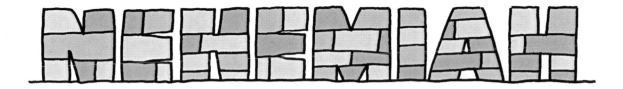

NEHEMIAH

Nehemiah was a man who led a group of Jewish exiles home to **Jerusalem** from Persia and (important bit, this) **rebuilt the city's walls.**

When we first meet him in chapter 1, Nehemiah is the **wine-taster** of the Persian King, **Artaxerxes**, which means that he was a high-flyer. The king gave him the OK to rebuild Jerusalem and made him governor of Judah. You can read all this in Nehemiah 1–2.

When it came to rebuilding Jerusalem, Nehemiah had **local enemies** who didn't want the city to become powerful again. They started by **mocking** the wall-builders...

The journey home for the exiles from Persia was no stroll... it was about 950 miles or 1520 km – which is 19 hours' driving at 50mph

Can you make building stones out of heaps of burned rubble?

Nehemiah 4:1–3

Even a fox could knock it down!

But the mockery soon turned into **threats, attacks, plots** on Nehemiah's life, and **false reports** to the king. Nehemiah succeeded because of his faith in God...

In the last chapters (11–13) Nehemiah leads a joyful procession round the new walls of Jerusalem – against all the odds, the Jewish people had returned home in style

Respect!

But now, God, make me strong!

Nehemiah's prayer

DISPUTED BOOKS

Some versions of the Bible have **fewer Old Testament books** than Catholic Bibles. If you look into a Protestant version of the Bible, you'll find that it usually has only **39** Old Testament books, rather than the **46** in Catholic Bibles.

So how did this happen?

Well, it's a tale of four Bibles...

1. A Greek Bible

Way back in about 250 BC, a group of Jewish scholars living in Alexandria, Egypt, decided to translate the Jewish scriptures **into Greek.** This was a great idea, as Greek in those days was like English is now, an international language, and most Jews of the time spoke it.

The translation they produced was called the **Septuagint**, and it was later used by the New Testament writers and by the early Christian church as the version of the Old Testament they knew best.

2. A Jewish Bible

In AD 90, a council of **Jewish rabbis** met at a place called Jamnia (near Jaffa in modern-day Israel) to agree **an official list** of the books in their scriptures. They rejected several books which appeared in the Septuagint, because the books weren't written in **Hebrew or Aramaic** like the oldest and most established books, but were more recent and in **Greek.**

So now there were two lists of books...

- **The longer Greek list** – which included all 46 books now in Catholic Bibles

- **The shorter Hebrew list** – which had only the 39 books now in Protestant Bibles

3. St Jerome's Vulgate

In the late 4th century AD **St Jerome** translated the Bible into Latin. He translated from the original **Hebrew scriptures**, and you'd think he would therefore only include the books on the shorter Hebrew list. But instead, he included all the books in the longer Greek list. His Latin Bible was called the **Vulgate** (meaning "popular") and was used for over 1,000 years. It established the longer list for the Catholic church.

Greek *Hebrew* *Latin*

St Jerome at his translator's desk, working from the Greek and Hebrew texts to produce his Latin Bible.

4. Martin Luther's Bible

Fast forward 1100 years to the 16th century, when the reformer **Martin Luther** was translating the Bible into German. Like St Jerome, Luther also worked from the Hebrew scriptures, but this time he used the shorter Hebrew list. He put the extra Greek books into a separate section, which he called the **Apocrypha** (a word meaning "hidden"). This set the trend for the Protestant family of churches.

> *Bibles used today by the Catholic and Orthodox churches have the longer list of books, and the extra books are called deutero-canonical (meaning a "second list" of books).*

The books

Here are the disputed books and sections which appear in Catholic Bibles, but not in Bibles which only use the shorter list. Introductions to the books are at the page numbers listed below.

Extra chapters in Esther (p. 101)

Tobit (p. 98)

1 & 2 Maccabees (p. 102)

Judith (p. 100)

Wisdom (p. 116)

Baruch (p. 127)

Sirach (p. 117)

Extra sections in Daniel (p. 132)

TOBIT

Tobit is a short book (it's a 20-minute read) and is a **folk tale** which the experts reckon was written in the 2nd century BC. The story revolves around **two people**: Tobit and Sarah (she was his relative, but lived a long way away).

*Meanwhile, **Sarah** has been married seven times, but on each wedding night her new husband has died before they had sexual relations. Everyone ridicules her because of it.*

Tobit is a good man. He gives to the poor, he prays, he looks after people in his community. But one day, disaster strikes and he goes blind.

Both Tobit and Sarah **pray to God** on the same day, weeping and **asking to die**. The two prayers arrive in heaven at the same time, and God sends one of his top seven angels, **Raphael**, on a secret mission to solve both Tobit and Sarah's problems at the same time.

The Book of **Tobit is significant** for at least two things:

■ Its beautiful **wedding prayer**, which affirms the nobility of marriage (in Tobit 8)

■ Its picture of a personal angel at work helped give rise to the whole idea of **guardian angels**

When you prayed, it was I who presented the record of your prayer before the Glory of the Lord.

The Angel Raphael reveals his true identity in Tobit 12:12

Angels

Angels appear throughout the Old and New Testaments, usually turning up in **human form**.

Yes, but what are angels?

Angels are **supernatural beings**, sent by God to do his work on earth. The English word "angel" comes from a Greek word, *angelos*, which means **messenger.**

Angels act as God's messengers, announcing good or bad news to individuals and groups of people. They also get **actively involved** in events, protecting God's people or attacking God's enemies.

In the Bible, angels are often mistaken for human beings

Not all angels are said to have wings, although the angels seen by the prophet Isaiah each had six wings (see Isaiah 6)

Angels are sometimes said to be too bright to look at

Some angels inspire awe and terror – "Fear not!" are often the first words they say

Here are some **big angelic moments** in the Bible...

☐ *Two angels rescue Abraham's nephew, Lot, from the doomed towns of Sodom and Gomorrah (Genesis 19)*

☐ *Jacob dreams of angels ascending and descending on a stairway to heaven (Genesis 28:12)*

☐ *The angel Gabriel tells Mary she will have a baby son and should call him Jesus (Luke 1:26-38)*

☐ *A host of angels appear to a group of Bethlehem shepherds announcing the birth of Jesus (Luke 2:8-14)*

☐ *An angel releases Peter from prison (Acts 12:1-10)*

judith

At the beginning of this book, the Israelites are in **dire trouble**. The **Assyrian** army, led by **Holofernes**, their fearsome commander-in-chief, is about to attack them. The only thing that stands in the Assyrians' way is the **small town of Bethulia**, which controls a strategic pass into Israel. The Assyrians besiege the town and cut off their **water supplies**, and soon the town is ready to give up.

Which is where Judith steps in.

> **Give me,** a **widow,** the strong **hand** to **execute my plan...** crush **their pride** by the **hand of a woman.**

*Judith's prayer
(Judith 9:9-10)*

Judith is a **beautiful young widow** who has been covering herself up in rough sackcloth ever since her husband died. But she has a cunning plan to save not only the people of Bethulia, but **the people of Israel**, too.

In the **male-dominated** world of the Old Testament, Judith stands for all the **Jewish women** who served God through their faith, courage and decisive action.

> *How can one woman single-handedly defeat a whole army?*

Read the book to find out! Judith has been loved from early times because of the quality of its storytelling. But read with care! Most of the historical details given in the book of Judith are wildly inaccurate.

ESTHER

The book of Esther, like the books of **Ezekiel** and **Daniel**, is set in the time of the **Jewish exile**. It tells the story of a Jewish woman called Esther, who married the Persian king and **saved her people** from being exterminated by their enemies.

There are four main characters in the story...

The book includes a 75-foot high gallows which plays a part in the surprise ending...

Judith, Esther and Ruth are the only three books in the Bible to be named after women...

This is the only biblical book which does not mention God...

King Xerxes (or "Ahasuerus" in older versions). He had powers of life and death over all his subjects.

Queen Esther, Xerxes' new wife. By her courage and quick-wittedness she averted disaster.

Haman, the Prime Minister, who planned to have all the Jews in the Persian empire killed.

Mordecai, cousin to Esther – with Esther's help, he turned Haman's threat into a Jewish triumph.

Every year, the scroll containing the book of Esther is read in full at a Jewish festival called Purim, celebrating hope and courage in the face of persecution

1 MACCABEES

The two books of Maccabees bring us closer to the time of Christ, covering the years 175-135 BC. The Jewish people were once again suffering under **foreign oppression**, but this time it wasn't the Babylonians or the Persians who were causing the problems, but **the Greeks**.

The Greek king, **Antiochus IV Epiphanes**, attacked the Temple in Jerusalem and set it up for the worship of false gods. He made it illegal for Jewish people to **sacrifice**, keep the **sabbath**, **circumcise** their male children and abstain from **eating pork**. Anyone who disobeyed was put to death.

1 Maccabees tells the story of a **family of rebels** who defied the king and fought back for their faith. The main characters in the family are shown below...

Mattathias – was a priest and the father of five sons. He started the revolt by refusing to worship Greek gods and killing a messenger of the king. He and the family fled into the desert, where different rebel groups joined them (see 1 Macc 2).

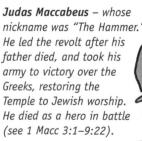

Judas Maccabeus – whose nickname was "The Hammer." He led the revolt after his father died, and took his army to victory over the Greeks, restoring the Temple to Jewish worship. He died as a hero in battle (see 1 Macc 3:1–9:22).

Jonathan – led his people after the death of Judas, fighting battles and making treaties. He was taken hostage and killed (see 1 Macc 9:23–12:53).

Simon – made a treaty with Rome which gave the Jews semi-independence from Greek rule. Simon founded a royal dynasty which continued until 37 BC (see 1 Macc 13-16).

THE BIBLE FROM SCRATCH

2 MACCABEES

So 2 Maccabees continues where 1 Maccabees left off, right?

Er, no. The author of 2 Maccabees zooms in on what happened in the middle years covered by 1 Maccabees. He tells us about events that aren't recorded in the first book.

In this book, the **persecution of the Jews** by the Greek king, Antiochus Epiphanes, continues. Two impressive chapters (6 and 7) have dramatic stories of **nonviolent resistance** by Jewish people. They are...

- **Eleazar** is put to death, even when he's offered a clever way out of his predicament (2 Maccabees 6:18-31)

- **Seven brothers and their mother** are also martyred and die making defiant speeches (2 Maccabees 7).

The author of the book isn't interested in merely telling us the news. He **adds his comments** on what is happening, praises or blames different people, and points out how **God was at work** behind the scenes through all the terrible and glorious events.

As you read the book, look out for **two themes** that are very important for the writer of 2 Maccabees. They are...

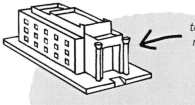

The Temple – the author tells his readers to guard and revere the Jerusalem Temple as the focus of their faith.

THE
LAW

The Law – the people should live according to the law of Moses. Then God won't allow them to suffer and be persecuted

POETRY

"Poetry and wisdom" doesn't even begin to describe the five wonderful books in the centre of the Bible. One of them asks some of the **hardest questions** about God, while another celebrates him in songs that hit the top notes of **joy**. One of them reads like a **sex manual**, while another complains that life is **absurd** and meaningless. Here they are...

Psalms – the hymn book of Israel, with 150 songs expressing faith, hope and love... and also fear, rage and despair

Job – this dramatic poem asks: how can God let good people suffer?

JOB   PROVERBS

Proverbs – a guide for how to live your life like a wise person rather than a fool, packed full of short, sharp (and often witty) sayings

PSALMS

SONG OF SONGS

Song of Songs – the Bible's one and only "the brakes are off" excursion into love and sex

Ecclesiastes – a sort of "bang your head against the wall" book – its subject is the absurdity of life

ECCLESI-ASTES   WISDOM

Wisdom – one of the great moments of the Jewish Wisdom tradition, with Greek philosophical flavoring

SIRACH

Sirach – practical and spiritual wisdom for how to lead a successful life, plus a unique tribute to the heroes of the Old Testament

INTRO

In this section we look at the seven books which take up **the center pages** of the Bible.

Five of them – Job, Proverbs, Ecclesiastes, Wisdom and Sirach – are known as **Wisdom books**...

... while the other two books contain **songs** (Psalms) and a **love poem** (Song of Songs). All seven books use poetry.

Poetry

The Hebrew people were a singing people. At several points the Old Testament **breaks into song**...

- **Moses** sings in Exodus 15
- **David** laments in 2 Samuel 1

The most famous book of Jewish poetry, the Psalms, is actually a **song book**. And the Hebrews were a hit, musically, in other countries...

Psalm 137:3

Sing us one of the songs of Zion!

Hebrew poetry is different from poetry as we know it – it **doesn't use rhyme**, for instance. Instead, it **plays with ideas** by repeating or expanding them, or turning them on their heads.

Here are **three ways** these ancient poets did it, all taken from one of the great psalms, **Psalm 55**...

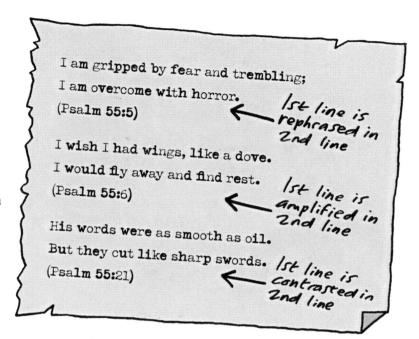

I am gripped by fear and trembling;
I am overcome with horror.
(Psalm 55:5)

1st line is rephrased in 2nd line

I wish I had wings, like a dove.
I would fly away and find rest.
(Psalm 55:6)

1st line is amplified in 2nd line

His words were as smooth as oil.
But they cut like sharp swords.
(Psalm 55:21)

1st line is contrasted in 2nd line

Wisdom

Hmm. Wisdom. It's that egghead philosophy stuff, isn't it?

Not really. The Wisdom books are just as interested in the practical question of **how to live wisely**, as in the big questions of **what life means**. There are **two kinds** of Wisdom books...

Proverbial – the book of Proverbs contains hundreds of two-line sayings that give smart advice for everyday life. See page 113.

Investigative – The book of Job uses dialogue and Ecclesiastes uses monologue to investigate the meaning of life, the purpose of suffering, etc. See pages 108 and 114.

The Wisdom books aim for the heart – the place where we do all our rational and ethical decision-making.

JOB

Ever asked yourself "why do good people suffer?" If so, Job's for you.

So what's it all about?

This famous book tells the story of a man called Job (rhymes with robe). He's a **good man** with a **big family**, lots of **friends**, a healthy **business** and respect for **God**.

And...?

Basically, **he loses it all**. Raiders steal his **camels**, lightning cooks all his **sheep**, a desert storm kills his **children**, and finally he's covered from head to foot with an epic case of **boils**. All this happens by chapter 2!

So not a great start, then?

Not really. In the rest of the book, **Job struggles** to find answers to his question: "How can God allow this to happen to me, a righteous man?" **Three friends** argue with him, giving the then-traditional answer to suffering: "If you suffer, it's because you've **sinned**".

Job trashes this argument and gets more and more **angry with God**. He ends up by challenging God to speak up and answer all his questions.

God replies!

God "answers" Job in chapters 38–41. He speaks out of a storm and gives a **firework display** of his power. He seems to be saying: "**Trust me**. I know what I'm doing!" Job's good fortunes are then restored.

THE TEMPLE

The Temple in Jerusalem was built by **Solomon** and destroyed when the army of **Babylon** sacked the city in 587 BC. Two further temples were built on the same site: first in **Nehemiah's** time and then by **King Herod** the Great in Jesus's time. This diagram shows Solomon's Temple, which stood when many of the psalms were written.

The Holy of Holies is where the ark of the covenant was kept. The high priest alone entered this space, probably once a year. A perfect cube, the room was lined in gold.

The Holy Place The Temple wasn't like a cathedral, where everyone can go inside. Only the priests were allowed in to carry out the rituals of worship and burn incense.

The courtyard is where the priests carried out animal sacrifices.

Storerooms and the priests' living space

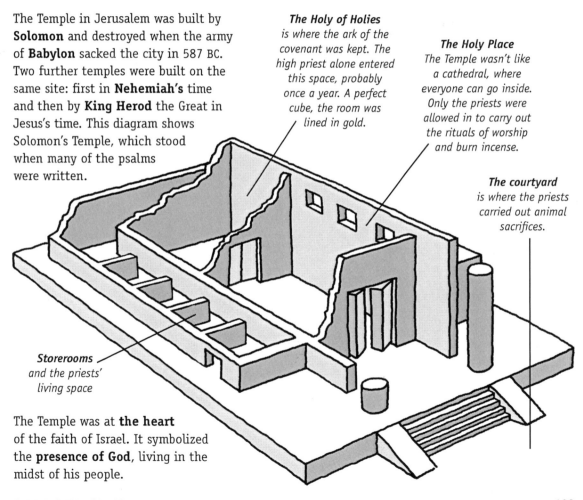

The Temple was at **the heart** of the faith of Israel. It symbolized the **presence of God**, living in the midst of his people.

Psalms

The book of Psalms is the longest book in the Bible, and it's also one of the Bible's high points. It contains 150 "psalms" (poems or songs). It's been used as a hymn and prayer book by Jews and Christians alike.

Having said that, some of the lyrics in the book of Psalms aren't exactly what you'd expect to find in a **church hymnbook**...

Play it again, Psalm...

You have put me in the lowest pit, in the darkest depths.
Psalm 88:6

The righteous will be glad when they bathe their feet in the blood of the wicked.
Psalm 58:10

Break the teeth in their mouths, O God!
Psalm 58:6

Awake, O Lord! Get up!
Psalm 44:23

It's hardly *Hymns of Incredible Niceness*, is it? The people who wrote the psalms weren't afraid to express their **fear, anger, despair, hatred and desire for revenge** to God... along with all the good, sunny feelings too. The psalms show us people **being real** with God.

> **So how were the psalms used?**

Some of the psalms were personal, **private prayers**. But many were clearly written for **worship** or prayer together. In the times of the Old Testament, this was done in the **Temple** in Jerusalem. Christians pray or sing the psalms in liturgy.

> **And what was this worship like?**

In a word, **noisy!** Some psalms are **quiet** and reflective, but on the whole the book is full of **shouting** and **dancing**, and Psalm 150 throws in trumpets, drums, harps, flutes and cymbals. Psalm 71:22–23 and Psalm 81:1–2 pictures what this worship was like.

The poetry

The psalms are bursting with **images** and **extravagant** poetic language.

In them, trees clap their hands, hills sing for joy, God's enemies melt like wax, the sun is like a sprinter, God rides on the clouds, and his law is sweeter than honey.

The poetry of the psalms is **powerful** and **inspiring**.

In the New Testament, **Jesus** quotes a lot from the psalms (some of **his last words** are from Psalm 22). The first **Christians** also knew the psalms by heart (see **Peter's** sermon in Acts 2). Christians have always valued this book more than any other part of the Old Testament.

> The Book of Psalms could well be called a 'little Bible' since it contains, set out in the briefest and most beautiful form, all that is to be found in the whole Bible.
>
> *Martin Luther*

Feel a bit daunted at the thought of wading through all 150 psalms? Make a start with this Top 20 list, which includes some of the best known. Put a check mark next to the numbers as you read them.

1
8
19
22
23
24
27
33
42
46
51
63
84
90
91
121
127
137
139
150

David

King David rates as one of the **best-known** and **best-loved** kings in history. He ruled ancient Israel between approximately 1010 and 970 BC. Here's the fast-forward version of his career...

1 SHEPHERD

As a young boy, David was in charge of his father's sheep. It was a **tough job.** He had to fight off wild animals who were hungry for a quick leg of lamb (see 1 Samuel 17:34–37).

2 SOLDIER

David had to **wait years** before he became king, and he spent them as a soldier. He was frequently on the run from **King Saul**, who wanted to kill him.

3 POET

David is famous as a songwriter. Several psalms reflect **his experiences**: 54 (on the run from **Saul**); 3 (on the run from his son, **Absalom**; and the famous Psalm 51 (where David says sorry after "**Bathshebagate**").

4 KING

David's early life is told in the book of 1 Samuel. He becomes king at the start of 2 Samuel. David ruled over a **golden age** in Israel, and he was later seen as a legendary figure, the **ideal ruler** for God's people. On the right are some of the key events of his reign. For more about David and his children, see page 84.

- *Becomes king, captures **Jerusalem** (2 Samuel 1 and 5)*
- *Brings **the ark** of Moses to Jerusalem (2 Samuel 6)*
- *Commits **adultery** and **murder** (2 Samuel 11–12)*
- *Fights off a **rebellion** by his son (2 Samuel 13–19)*
- ***Dies** (1 Kings 2)*

Guess what *he* got for Christmas!

PROVERBS

Only your friends will tell you when your face is dirty.	*When elephants fight it is the grass that suffers.*	*A book is like a garden carried in a pocket.*	*Fashion is more powerful than any tyrant.*	*Those that lie down with dogs, get up with fleas.*
Sicilian	**Kikuyu**	**Chinese**	**Latin**	**Blackfoot**

What's a proverb? It's a **short saying** which is easy to memorize and easy to repeat when needed. Traditional cultures (such as the ones above) treasured their proverbs. They were a **fund of wisdom** which were used by **ordinary people** to make everyday decisions, and also by **judges** to decide legal cases. The Bible's book of Proverbs is a big collection of ancient Jewish wise sayings.

So what's the big theme of the book?

Proverbs is a **guide** to successful living. It gives lots of practical advice on **how to be wise** and what to do in different situations.

And it's written by King Solomon?

Many of the proverbs are credited to Solomon, although the book draws its sayings from many different sources. You can find these assorted proverbs from **chapter 10** onwards.

The proverb-makers wanted their sayings to stick in the mind. So they used **memory-tricks**...

■ See Proverbs 30:15–31 for sayings using **lists of numbers**.

■ In Proverbs 31:10–31 (which is a poem) the first letter of each new verse starts with the next letter of the **Hebrew alphabet**.

■ Many Proverbs use **comedy**. Once you've read and laughed at them, they stay with you!

ECCLESIASTES

This is written by a guy who called himself 'the preacher', right?

Yes, but he can also be called 'the philosopher'. The book is basically a rant about the meaning of life and how everything seems to be absurd.

Ecclesiastes starts off on a **low note**...

> It is useless, useless, said the philosopher. Life is useless, all useless. You spend your life working and what do you have to show for it?

Ecclesiastes 1:2

And then it **gets worse**. If the book of Proverbs is generally **optimistic** about life, then Ecclesiastes is generally **pessimistic**.

THE SEARCH

The philosopher tries to find **happiness** and **meaning** in laughter, enjoyment, riches and religion. But **they all fail**. In the end, **death** makes them all meaningless.

Even God seems **unjust** and **unpredictable**. "I will suffer the same fate as fools. So what have I gained from being so wise?" (Ecclesiastes 2:15).

All this raises the question: **why** is such a negative, despairing book **in the Bible** at all? It's a question that's often been asked by Jewish and Christian experts. Here are some of their answers...

■ the book has a strong theme of our **dependence** on God.
■ **doubt** is valued by God and can help to **shape faith**.
■ it's no good ignoring the **bad things** that happen in life – we need to face them honestly.

Song of Songs

The Bible has its boring moments, but this isn't one of them. The book is a steamy **love poem**. Here's the story...

It's spring. In dazzlingly beautiful countryside, while the flowers grow and the foxes run, **two young lovers** celebrate their love in a series of songs. The songs are intensely **passionate**, with rich **physical** and **sexual** imagery.

Really? Do you have any... er... examples?

Yes – but **don't try this at home.** Here's how the two lovers talk about each other...

Her hair... is like a flock of goats

His lips... are like lilies

Quotes from Song of Songs 5, 6 and 7

His legs... are pillars of marble

Her navel... is like a goblet of wine

Her nose... is like the tower of Lebanon

... all of which might sound a bit **bizarre**, but that's how people talked in those days when they were in love. The Song of Songs is an **Eastern love poem**, not a scene from a Hollywood movie.

So what's all this doing in the Bible then?

Maybe it's to show the high value that God gives to **sexual love.** After all, he invented it in the first place.

WISDOM

The Book of Wisdom (aka the Wisdom of Solomon) was written around 50 BC in the city of **Alexandria, Egypt.** That makes it the last of all the Old Testament books to be written.

Jewish people settled in Alexandria in large numbers from the time the city was founded, almost 300 years earlier. The city was **second only to Rome** in the ancient world, and it may be that the writer of the Book of Wisdom was concerned that his fellow-Jews had fallen under the spell of the **Greek** way of life that was dominant at that time, and had forgotten their **Jewish heritage.**

The Book of Wisdom is divided into **three parts...**

Be wise!

(Wisdom 1:1–6:21) Evil people think they can behave as they want, saying there'll be no payback once they're dead, but they're wrong! They'll have to face a reckoning for their sins. Meanwhile, "the souls of the just are in the hands of God, and no torment shall touch them" (Wisdom 3:1).

Praise for wisdom

(Wisdom 6:22–11:1) Speaking in the voice of King Solomon, the author praises wisdom and prays that God will send him wisdom from his heavenly throne.

God's goodness

(Wisdom 11:2–19:22) The author now speaks to God, praising him for his unfailing goodness to the Israelites in the past. He especially recalls the Exodus from Egypt, which must have reminded his readers in Alexandria not to forget the dangers of living in Egypt – and not to forget the God who saved them from slavery.

Sirach

Sirach (aka **Ecclesiasticus**) is mostly a book of practical, **down-to-earth wisdom**, written by someone with great knowledge of the human heart. Sirach offers his words of wisdom to parents and children, husbands and wives, the young and the old, as well as to business partners, friends, employees, politicians, and many others.

The book of Sirach also includes a unique tribute to **the heroes** of the Old Testament (see Sirach chapters 44-50). Sirach has always been a **popular read**, and many of its verses have been frequently quoted. Such as...

BIG BOOK ALERT

With 51 chapters, Sirach is in the Top 10 biggest books of the Bible, coming in at No. 8. See page 29 for the full list.

> *Read me the bits that talk about life after death.*

> *Um...*

Unlike the Book of Wisdom, Sirach never mentions the possibility of life after death, or considers the idea that God might reward good people and punish bad people beyond death.

Instead, Sirach's interest is in the world of here and now. For him, good is always rewarded and evil is always punished in this life. He never asks the question: why do good people suffer? If you want a book which does that, turn back to the book of Job (see page 108)!

> *Has anyone who ever trusted in the Lord been disappointed?*
>
> Sirach 2:10

> *Come then, praise the God of the universe, who everywhere works great wonders.*
>
> Sirach 50:22

PROPHETS

Isaiah – God's in control of the nations

Jeremiah – the original prophet of doom

Lamentations – grieving over the smoking ruins of Jerusalem

Baruch – hope in the darkest days of Babylon

Daniel – a Jewish prophet in the court of Babylon

Ezekiel – the wild man among the prophets

They had **dreams and visions**. They ranted on street corners. They were angry at the **injustices** they saw around them. And they had to have courage. The prophets **spoke for God** in the dark days before and after Israel and Judah went into exile. These 18 amazing books record their **revolutionary** messages.

Nahum – dances on the grave of the Assyrian empire

Habakkuk – How can God stand the Babylonians?

Zephaniah – it's judgment day!

Obadiah – doom to the Edomites!

Micah – God hates fake religion

Hosea – God's love for his wayward people

Haggai – stop slacking and rebuild God's temple!

Joel – a plague of locusts is a picture of God's judgment

Amos – God's on the side of the poor

Jonah – the Bible meets "Jaws"

Zechariah – amazing visions in the night

Malachi – a big telling-off for God's people

INTRO

Who were the prophets?

The first of the prophets appear in the history books of the Old Testament. There are extensive (and exciting) stories about the two main prophets during the early era of the kings: **Elijah** and **Elisha** (see pages 87 and 91).

But the **later prophets**, such as Isaiah, Ezekiel and Amos, aren't mentioned in the history books. Instead they have **their own books** in the prophecy section at the end of the Old Testament, even though a number of them lived during the time covered by the books of 1 and 2 Kings.

The books of the prophets are roughly arranged with the **biggest** books at the **front**. Isaiah has 66 chapters, while Obadiah has only one.

There's another difference too. Some of the prophets were **men of action**, while others are known for their **words of prophecy**. If you're making a start in reading the prophets, here are some whose lives are an **interesting read**...

- **Elijah** – see 1 Kings 17 – 2 Kings 2
- **Elisha** – see 2 Kings 2–7
- **Daniel** – see Daniel 1–6
- **Jonah** – see the whole of Jonah

So what did the prophets do? Predict the future, presumably?

The prophets did talk about the future, but mainly to **warn people** what would happen if they kept disobeying the law of God. Talking about the future wasn't their main job. They were called to speak **God's messages** to Israel and Judah, when both nations had turned away from him.

The prophets were **dissidents**. They spoke out when they believed the king, his advisers, judges, priests and even the ordinary people were going wrong. And they spoke **in the name of God**. 'This is what the Lord says' was one of their catchphrases.

Here are some of the things **they attacked**...

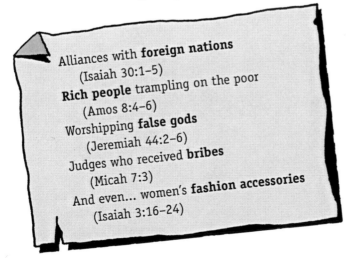

Alliances with **foreign nations**
(Isaiah 30:1–5)
Rich people trampling on the poor
(Amos 8:4–6)
Worshipping **false gods**
(Jeremiah 44:2–6)
Judges who received **bribes**
(Micah 7:3)
And even... women's **fashion accessories**
(Isaiah 3:16–24)

Naturally, none of this made the prophets very **popular**. Here's a taste of their experience...

They will despise you; it will be like living among scorpions.

God calls Ezekiel (2:6)

This man must be put to death!

About Jeremiah (38:4)

Jerusalem, Jerusalem! You kill the prophets God has sent you!

Jesus in Luke 13:34

Was there any prophet that your ancestors did not persecute?

Stephen in Acts 7:52

*It was only later that people came to see how **courageous** the prophets had been, and that their messages had been **inspired by God**. Their writings were collected and included in the growing canon of **scripture**.*

ISAIAH

Isaiah. Who was he?

Name: Isaiah, son of Amoz

Occupation: Prophet to Judah

Career: Called to be a prophet in the year King Uzziah died (see Isaiah 6). Prophesied in Jerusalem for 40 years

Other info: Reputed to be of royal blood. Possibly killed by King Manasseh

And did this Isaiah write Isaiah the book?

That's not such a stupid question as it looks! Here's the issue...

Chapters 1–39
contain prophecies given before Judah was taken into exile.

Chapters 40–66
describe in detail events during and after the exile, 150 years later.

Some people believe God enabled Isaiah son of Amoz to **see into the future** in this detailed way. Others think it's more likely that chapters 40–66 were the work of Isaiah's **later disciples**, writing during and after the exile.

If this second option is correct, the later chapters came from people who closely followed Isaiah's teaching. The whole book therefore has a unity of **thought**, even if it doesn't have a unity of **authorship**.

The book of Isaiah is unique among the prophets in covering the time **before** the exile and the time **after** it. As you'd expect, the three parts of the book have different **moods and messages**...

> **You are doomed! You will be carried away as prisoners. Your leaders will starve to death and the common people will die of thirst.**

Gloom and doom in Isaiah 5:13

Gloom & doom

In part one (**Isaiah 1–39**), Isaiah attacks the situation in **Judah before the exile**. Jerusalem had become a wealthy city, and the rich were **oppressing the poor** and helpless. Also, because of the threat of foreign invasion, Judah had made a number of **treaties** with nations that followed false gods.

Isaiah said that **God was angry** with all this and would punish his people for breaking faith with him.

Hope & warning

In part two (**Isaiah 40-55**), the message changes dramatically to give **hope and comfort** for the exiles of Judah who were living in captivity in Babylon. In part three (**Isaiah 56-66**), the prophet gives **messages of warning** to the returned exiles.

One theme in all these chapters is that God controls everything that goes on in the world. Far from being the tribal god of Israel, he is "**the everlasting God**, the Creator of the ends of the earth" (Isaiah 40:28).

> **Jerusalem, be strong and great again! Holy city of God, clothe yourself with splendour! The heathen will never enter your gates again.**

Hope and glory in Isaiah 52:1

Two of the most famous chapters in the book are Isaiah 53 and 61. Isaiah 53 seems to point forward to the death of Jesus, over 500 years later. And Isaiah 61 was quoted by Jesus in Luke 4:16–30 at the start of his work.

JEREMIAH

The prophets were **unpopular.** The prophets were **hated.** But Jeremiah was the most unpopular and hated of them all.

Trying to get our sympathy? Forget it! Jeremiah was a traitor! He was downright unpatriotic!

TRAITOR!

That's how Jeremiah was seen in his time. He had to tell the people of Judah that God was going to punish their sins – that the mighty **Babylonians** would destroy their nation and smash **Jerusalem**, the city they loved.

And when the Babylonians did attack, while everyone else was trying to keep morale up, Jeremiah told them to **give in** and **accept God's judgment**. He was beaten, imprisoned, thrown into a muddy cistern, threatened with death, etc.

Poor Jeremiah! I wonder how he felt about it all...

He wanted to **give up.** Sometimes things got so bad that he moaned to God, but it was no use...

When I say, "I will forget the Lord and no longer speak in his name," then your message is like a fire burning deep within me. I try my best to hold it in, but can no longer keep it back.

Jeremiah 20:9

THE BIBLE FROM SCRATCH

So how long was Jeremiah a prophet?

Forty years – and he saw his worst prophecies fulfilled. The book of Jeremiah records his amazing **life** and **message**, mixing his prophecies with events in his life. Here are two ways into this great book...

What he said...

Jeremiah had an urgent message to put across. So he often used **pictures** and **dramatic actions** to drive his words home. Here are some of them (numbers below = chapters in Jeremiah)...

■ the potter making a pot (18)
■ the smashed pot (19)
■ good figs and bad figs (24)
■ the wooden and iron yokes (27 and 28)

Jeremiah's enemies may have hated his words, but they couldn't forget them!

Although Jeremiah had a tough message to preach, when the **disasters** he had predicted started to happen, he began to speak about **hope for the future.** God's punishment wouldn't last for ever, he said.

In the greatest passage of the book (Jeremiah 31:31–34) Jeremiah looks forward to a **new agreement** with God, when (God says): "I will put my law in their minds and write it on their hearts."

What he did...

Here are some of the **main events** in Jeremiah's life...

■ called to be a prophet by God (1)
■ arrested! (26)
■ the Babylonians lay siege to Jerusalem and Jeremiah buys a field (32)
■ in the siege, he is imprisoned (37)
■ he is flung into a muddy cistern and left to die (38)
■ Jerusalem falls to the Babylonians (39)
■ he is taken by force to Egypt (40–43)

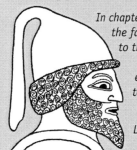

In chapter 39, Jeremiah witnesses the fall of Jerusalem in 587 BC to the fearsome army of King Nebuchadnezzar and the exile of the Jewish people to Babylon. It seemed like the end for God's people.

Left: a Babylonian soldier.

LAMENTATIONS

Lamentations marks one of the emotional **extreme points** of the Bible. It's a collection of **five poems** (one per chapter) agonizing over the destruction of Jerusalem by the Babylonian army. The poems were probably written very soon after the **fall of the city**. The person who wrote them was almost certainly an eyewitness to the **horror** of it all.

Here are some of the book's themes ←

ANGST – the poems use short sentences in a kind of **sobbing rhythm** to lament over the ruined city. The death and destruction is described in **vivid detail**, and the enemies mock: "Is this that lovely city? Is this the pride of the world?" (Lamentations 2:15).

CONFESSION – so is all this misery an accident or twist of fate? No, it's a **punishment** sent by God: "We have sinned and rebelled, and you, O Lord, have not forgiven us" (Lamentations 3:42). The poems don't blame God but uphold his **goodness**.

HOPE & DESPAIR – amazingly, despite the trauma and grief, Lamentations manages to **keep faith** with God – even though the hope of the writer is often eclipsed by **despair**. Here's his often-quoted expression of faith: "The Lord's unfailing love and mercy still continue..." (Lamentations 3:22).

The book closes with this **prayer of desperation**...

> *Bring us back to you, Lord! Bring us back!*
> *Restore our ancient glory.*
> *Or have you rejected us for ever?*
> *Is there no limit to your anger?*

Lamentations 5:21–22

BARUCH

Who wrote this one?

Well, it's a bit of a story. Baruch was a disciple of the prophet Jeremiah and was with him when the Babylonians captured Jerusalem and destroyed its temple. Experts think the book of Baruch wasn't actually written by Baruch, but by someone living later who admired him and wanted the book to follow the tradition of Jeremiah (for more info, see page 225).

The opening verses of Baruch tell us the book was read out to the **Jewish exiles** living in **Babylon** (see page 130 for more info about the exile). The heart of the book has **three sections**...

1. "We have sinned" (Baruch 1:15–3:8) Here are heartfelt prayers of confession for the sins which brought disaster on the Jewish people.

Each one of us went after the devices of our own wicked hearts, served other gods and did evil in the sight of the Lord, our God.

Baruch 1:22

He who dismisses the light, and it departs, calls it, and it obeys him trembling... Such is our God; no other is to be compared to him.

Baruch 3:33, 36

2. "Such is our God" (Baruch 3:9–4:4) In beautiful poetry, Baruch praises the wisdom of God, given to the people of Israel in the Law of Moses.

3. "Fear not, my people!" (Baruch 4:5–5:9) These four poems, each beginning with the words, "Fear not!", are calculated to put fresh heart into the exiles, promising an end to the exile.

Look to the east, Jerusalem! Behold the joy that comes to you from God. Here come your sons whom you once let go.

Baruch 4:36-37

EZEKIEL

If there were a prize for **Weirdest Prophet** of the Old Testament, then Ezekiel would pick up the Lifetime Achievement award. His **strange visions** and the way he acted out his prophecies (for example, by tying himself up, or lying on his side for 40 days) make him seem **eccentric**, to say the least.

His book starts off as it means to go on. By the banks of one of the rivers in **Babylon** he has one of the strangest and most mind-blowing **visions of God** in the whole Bible. This is how his vision begins...

I looked, and I saw a windstorm coming out of the north – an immense cloud with flashing lightning and surrounded by brilliant light. The center of the fire looked like glowing metal, and in the fire was what looked like four living creatures...

Ezekiel 1:4–5

The vision continues with **wheels** (filled with eyes) turning inside other wheels, and a sapphire **throne** above them, and...

well, you get the picture. All of which has been variously explained as an encounter with a **UFO**, the result of taking hallucinatory **drugs**, or that the old boy was **just plain nuts**.

However, the book of Ezekiel tells us that this was a genuine **revelation of God** himself: "This was the appearance of the likeness of the glory of the Lord. When I saw it, I fell face down..." (Ezekiel 1:28).

128

Ezekiel is one of the prophets who spoke to the Jewish **exiles in Babylon** (Daniel was one of the others). He had been taken there with a group of leaders from Jerusalem in in 597 BC, **11 years** before the city was finally destroyed by the Babylonians. The first part of his book has prophecies that were given before Jerusalem fell. Here's the sequence...

Looking for a map of Babylon? See page 134.

BABYLON

Chapters 1–32
messages of **doom**

JERUSALEM FALLS
587 BC

Chapters 33–48
messages of **hope**

After Jerusalem was destroyed, Ezekiel's message **switched to hope.** The exiles were traumatized and in despair at the loss of their heritage. They were asking **questions** such as...

Where was God when Jerusalem was destroyed?

There's no hope for us now – is there?

The gods of Babylon must be more powerful than the Lord. After all, they defeated him!

Some highlights

- God calls Ezekiel to be a prophet (1–3)
- Ezekiel acts out the siege of Jerusalem (4)
- The false shepherds of Israel (34)
- "I will put my spirit in you" (36:24–38)
- The valley of the dry bones (37)

Ezekiel responded with a **sequence of prophecies...**

God's purpose – like the other prophets, Ezekiel emphasized that the people of Judah had been exiled because of their sins.

Returning home – he said there was hope in the future for them, because God would bring them back to their own land.

Sovereign Lord – like Isaiah (see page 122) he gave them a vision of God as utterly powerful and transcendent.

THE EXILE

In 597 BC, disaster fell upon **Judah**. Babylon, the superpower of that time, overran the country and took all the **leading citizens** into exile in **Babylonia**, 950 miles from home. The Jewish people, who had once been slaves in Egypt, were now **slaves once again**.

Why did it happen?

For **many reasons** – political, military and religious. Here's how some of the people who were actually involved in the events surrounding the exile saw it...

> Because the nation was corrupt! The rich made slaves of the poor, and the leaders misled the people...
>
> *Isaiah*

> Because Judah wouldn't give up the worship of false gods!
>
> *Jeremiah*

> Because the King of Judah had rebelled against my rule. He needed to be taught a lesson!
>
> *Nebuchadnezzar, Emperor of Babylon*

The exile of Judah took place in **two stages**...

597 BC

King Jehoiachin and others (including the prophet Ezekiel) went into exile in Babylon.

587 BC

The same thing happened to King Zedekiah. This time, Jerusalem was totally destroyed.

Behind all these reasons, the prophets saw **the hand of God**. It was God, they said, who was **punishing** the people of Judah for their sins.

And how did they live in exile?

Jeremiah the prophet wrote to one of the first groups of exiles (see Jeremiah 29) telling them to **settle down**. Here's what he told them (see right)...

Build houses and settle down. Plant gardens and eat what you grow in them. Marry and have children. Then let them get married, so that they also may have children. You must increase in numbers and not decrease. Work for the good of the cities where I have made you go as prisoners. Pray to **me** on their behalf, because if they are prosperous, you will be prosperous too...

But even for those exiles who lived prosperously in Babylon (and many didn't) there was **despair**. Nothing could take away the pain of losing the **land** they loved.

Almost **70 years** after the first Judeans had been taken captive, the exile began to come to an end. The **Babylonian** empire (which had conquered the Assyrian empire) was in turn conquered by the **Persians**, who allowed the exiled peoples they had inherited to **go home**.

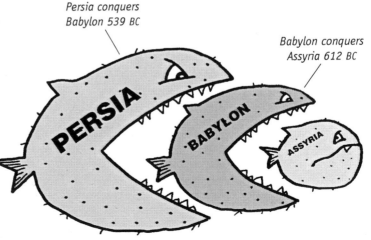

Persia conquers Babylon 539 BC

Babylon conquers Assyria 612 BC

PERSIA

BABYLON

ASSYRIA

Daniel

Daniel is like **two books in one**. There are two distinct types of material, one telling stories, the other revealing visions...

Stories – chapters 1–6 and 13-14 tell the adventures of Daniel and his friends, a group of young Jewish exiles, training for top jobs in the royal court of Babylon. The stories are famous, including Daniel in the lions' den.

Visions – meanwhile, over in chapters 7–12, something entirely different is going on. These chapters record a series of strange visions which predict the future in coded imagery.

Stories

In these chapters (Daniel 1–6 and 13-14), **young Daniel** rises quickly to a key position in the royal court at Babylon. He was there for nearly 70 years – throughout the **whole Jewish exile**. Like **Joseph** (in Genesis 41), Daniel became successful by interpreting the king's dreams.

The Daniel stories aren't just entertainment. They were written to **encourage** Jewish people facing hard times under harsh, foreign rulers who wanted them to give up their faith. These chapters in Daniel tell them to **stick with it**.

One of the great stories in Daniel is Belshazzar's feast in chapter 5, which gave us the expression, 'the writing on the wall'.

Visions

Daniel's visions are in a **form of prophecy** known as **apocalyptic**. One of the big features of this type of prophecy is that it uses **complex symbolism** to reveal what God is doing behind the scenes of human history. Here's the symbolism found in Daniel's three visions...

Vision 1

Daniel sees four strange beasts, representing four empires. They are judged by God, who gives power to a glorious 'Son of Man'.
Daniel 7

Vision 2

Daniel sees a goat defeat a ram. The goat (which represents a great empire) has four horns. One of the horns grows a little horn that causes havoc for God's people.
Daniel 8

Vision 3

A glorious figure appears to Daniel and gives a detailed prediction of the future.
Daniel 10-12

OK... but what's it all about?

The answers to that question are much argued-over. There are **two main theories**, each claiming that Daniel's visions are about...

■ **Events happening at the time** – Daniel is describing (not predicting) events which took place around 200 years before Jesus lived, intending to give the people hope.

■ **Events to come either now or in the future** – ever since the time of Jesus, people have claimed that Daniel is speaking about events in their own time. This approach is generally not taken by Catholics.

See Zechariah, parts of Ezekiel, and Revelation for more apocalyptic.

HOSEA

This is the story of a **broken marriage**. Hosea and Gomer got married and had three children. But then Gomer was **unfaithful** several times over and left home to be with her lovers. Even though she was a prostitute, Hosea **still loved her** and eventually made her his wife again. You can read all this in Hosea 1–3.

Through this crisis in his life, Hosea gained a deep insight into how God saw **Israel's unfaithfulness** to him. Hosea's broken marriage became a picture of God's relationship with his people...

> *Israel, I will make you my wife. I will be true and faithful...*

God speaking in Hosea 2:19

Hosea was prophet to the northern kingdom of **Israel** about the same time **Isaiah** was in the south (see map on page 141). He had a hard message to deliver. Because of the people's sins, Israel would be **swallowed up by war**.

So there was no hope, then?

Surprisingly, there was hope in Hosea's message. Just as Hosea took his wife back, so God could **never forget** his people. The book's most hopeful words are...

> *How can I give you up, Israel? How can I abandon you? My heart won't let me do it. My love for you is too strong.*

God speaking in Hosea 11:8

JOEL

The prophet Joel probably lived some time between 500 and 300 BC, when the Jewish people were settled in **their land again** after the exile was over. Joel's book opens with a terrible **plague of locusts** that had turned the land into a desert.

Judgment!

However, Joel wasn't just a reporter on a locust disaster. He saw the locusts as a picture of what God's **judgment** would be like at the end of history. Like the locusts, he says, God's judgment will be...

- **A day of darkness**
- **The end of God's blessings** – as everything good is destroyed
- **Unstoppable** – you can't swat a swarm of locusts, and you can't stop God's anger

This vision of judgment, says Joel, should **turn us back** to God. Then he will restore the good things we have lost because of our sins. Joel also foresees a time when God will **give his Spirit** to all people, rather than to just a chosen few in the Old Testament. The most famous words from his book were quoted on the **Day of Pentecost**, when the Spirit fell on the first Christian believers...

Did you know? The average swarm of locusts can devour 900 square miles of vegetation per day...

> I will pour out my Spirit on all people. Your sons and daughters will prophesy, your old men will dream dreams, your young men will see visions.

Joel 2:28

AMOS

Amos was just a **shepherd** from Judah until God called him. He was told to leave his sheep, go north to **Israel** and preach a very tough, dangerous message to the people there. The call was powerful...

> The lion has roared – Who will not fear? The Sovereign Lord has spoken – who can but prophesy?
>
> *Amos 3:8*

Although his book is quite short, Amos was one of the **fiercest and greatest** of the Old Testament prophets. He prophesied in Israel around 760 BC and was one of the group of four 8th-century prophets, all of them famous for their **ethical teaching** – the other three were **Isaiah**, **Micah** and **Hosea**.

So what was his message about?

Here's the background. On the surface, everything seemed fine. Israel, under the rule of **King Jeroboam II**, was enjoying a rare period of peace and plenty. Trade was up. The shekel was doing nicely. Mansions were being built. Even religion was booming.

But as Amos pointed out, these good times were only for the **wealthy few.** While the rich and powerful enjoyed life, **the poor** went hungry or sold themselves into slavery.

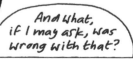

> And what, if I may ask, was wrong with that?

What made it worse was that the rich were **outwardly very religious**. They even believed their riches were a blessing from God. They didn't think for a moment that there was a giant contradiction between the way they **worshipped** and the way they **abused the poor**.

Amos is **ferocious** like no one else in the Bible in his attacks on the corruption, injustice and oppression he sees all around him. His book **burns with anger**.

He tells his listeners that Israel will be **wiped out** and that God will hunt every last one of them down, even if they hide in the heavens or on the bottom of the sea (Amos 9:2–4). His language throughout the book is **extreme**.

Here's Amos's brutal attack on the **religion of the rich**...

> I hate, I **despise** your **religious feasts**; I cannot stand your assemblies... Away with the noise of your songs! I **will** not **listen** to **the music of your harps.** But **let** justice roll on **like** a **river, righteousness** like a never-failing stream!

Amos 5:21, 23–24

Amos's cry for justice has had a **big impact** in modern times. Many Christians who campaign against **local** and **global injustice** root their action in his teaching. His words still speak powerfully for the poor and oppressed.

Was not Jesus an extremist for love? Was not Amos an extremist for justice? Was not Paul an extremist for the gospel of Jesus Christ?

Martin Luther King Jr, Letter from Birmingham Jail, 1963

Obadiah

It's the **shortest book** in the Old Testament. There aren't even any chapters – only verses. And it's pretty **bad-tempered**. Obadiah thunders against **Edom**, a kingdom to the south of Judah, and gleefully predicts its downfall.

Can you tell me why exactly he does that?

Um... how long have you got? It's one of those Middle East conflicts.

BAD BLOOD

Israel and Edom went back a long way. Right back to **Jacob** and his brother **Esau** in the book of Genesis. Israel was descended from Jacob, Edom from Esau. The two nations constantly **feuded** throughout the Old Testament.

Saul fought them, David conquered them, but the Edomites continued to be a thorn in Judah's side, **invading or rebelling** with boring regularity.

TREACHERY

Then in 587 BC came the final blow: Babylon razed Jerusalem. Instead of helping their brother nation, the Edomites **sided with the Babylonians**. They handed over escaping Judeans, looted the fallen city and gloated over the whole tragedy.

DOOM

For Obadiah, this is **payback time**. He pronounces doom on Edom for their treachery. The Edomites thought they were unbeatable. Their kingdom was on top of a mountain approached through a narrow canyon – the perfect defence! But Obadiah says they'll be **ransacked** and **destroyed**.

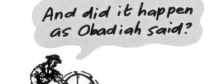

And did it happen as Obadiah said?

Yes. By the 5th century BC, Edom had fallen to Arab invaders.

WHO WAS WHERE?

The prophets whose books are in this section of the Bible spoke between the **8th** and **5th** centuries BC in **Israel**, **Judah** and the exile in **Babylon**. This chart shows where they were.

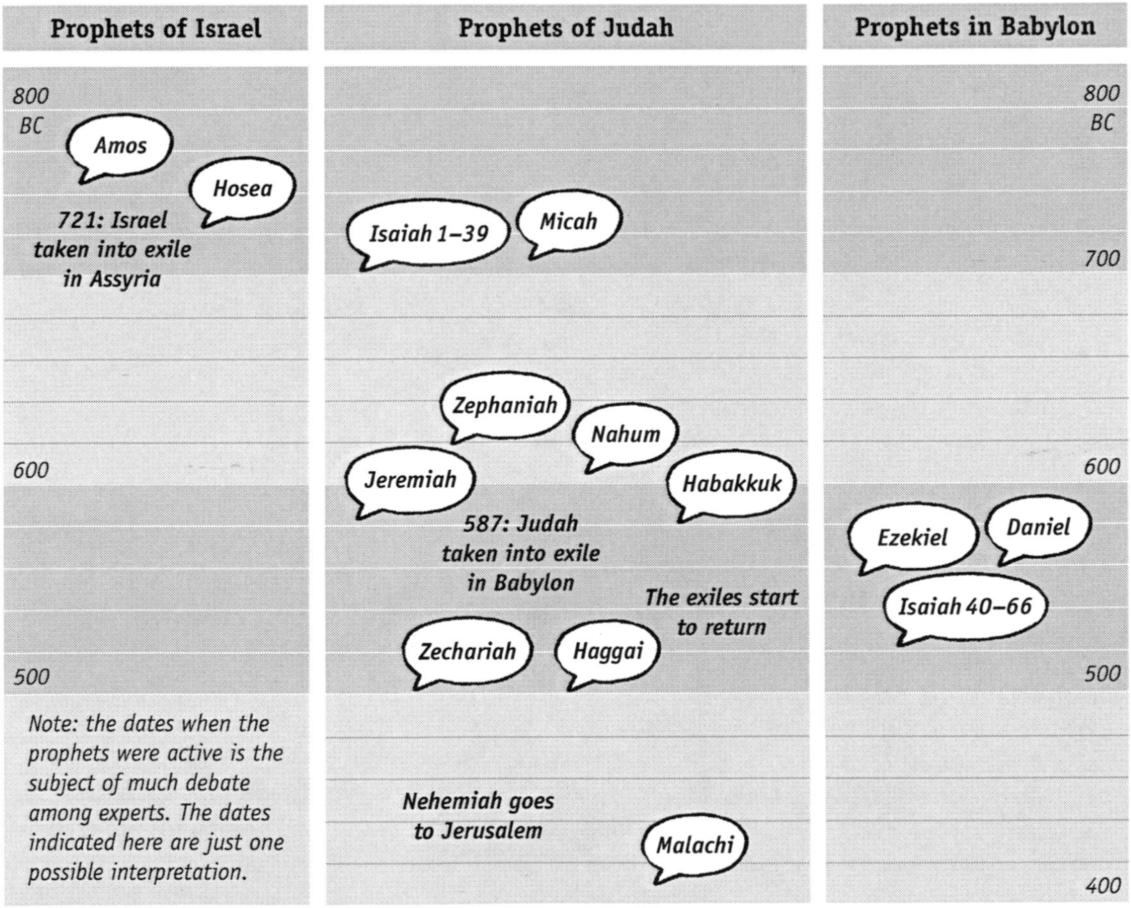

Prophets of Israel	Prophets of Judah	Prophets in Babylon

Prophets of Israel

800 BC

Amos

Hosea

721: Israel taken into exile in Assyria

600

500

Note: the dates when the prophets were active is the subject of much debate among experts. The dates indicated here are just one possible interpretation.

Prophets of Judah

Isaiah 1–39   Micah

Zephaniah

Nahum

Jeremiah   Habakkuk

587: Judah taken into exile in Babylon

The exiles start to return

Zechariah   Haggai

Nehemiah goes to Jerusalem

Malachi

Prophets in Babylon

800 BC

700

600

Ezekiel   Daniel

Isaiah 40–66

500

400

JONAH

Jonah **didn't want** to be a prophet. He wasn't alone in this – **Jeremiah** also tried to turn down the job (see page 124). But Jonah actively tried to get out of the prophecy business – and this book tells his story.

It all started when **God told Jonah**...

GO TO NINEVEH!

God wanted the people of **Nineveh** (the Assyrian capital) to turn from their evil ways. But Jonah **wouldn't go** to deliver the message. Like other people of his time, he **hated the Assyrians** for their cruelty. He wanted God to destroy them – not forgive them.

Nineveh has more than 120,000 people who can't tell their right hand from their left, and many cattle as well. Should I not be concerned about that great city?

God speaking in Jonah 4:11

So Jonah caught a ship going in the **opposite direction** from Nineveh. But God wouldn't take no for an answer. Jonah ended up in the stomach of a **great fish** which was heading – you guessed it – in the direction of Nineveh.

The book of Jonah is interesting for the unexpected way it breaks down **racial prejudice**. It reveals that God's concern isn't limited to one racial group – the **Jewish** people – but extends as far as the **Assyrians**, the biggest enemies of Israel at the time. This message is also carried by the book of **Ruth** (see page 78).

micah

Micah was one of a group of **four great prophets** who spoke out during the 8th century BC...

Amos and Hosea prophesied in the northern kingdom of Israel

Samaria

Jerusalem

Micah and Isaiah prophesied in the southern kingdom of Judah

In Micah's time, Judah and Israel were as bad as the nations next door. These nations believed that if their gods were given the right amount of animal (and human) **sacrifices** and **religious rituals**, then the gods would repay them with rain, good harvests and success in battle. It was like a deal: 'You give me x and I'll see you're all right.'

— *Thanks!*

Judah and Israel had come to believe that they had the same sort of deal going with God. As long as they kept doing the religious stuff, they could **live how they liked** and God would be OK with it.

Micah spoke out against this cosy arrangement. His great theme is that God is a **God of justice**. God expects **the rich** and powerful to show justice in the way they treat **the poor** and weak. He doesn't want thousands of animal sacrifices. He doesn't want empty, mechanical "worship". Instead...

> **66** What does the lord require of you? To act justly and to love mercy and to walk humbly with your God. **99**

Micah 6:8

NAHUM

If you were living in the Middle East in the time of Nahum, then you were in the shadow of **Assyria**, the undisputed superpower of the region.

Assyria was **active and violent**. The people of Judah saw Assyria take over **27,000** Israelites into exile in 721 BC, when the city of Samaria fell. Twenty years later, another **200,000** people went when the Assyrians invaded Judah.

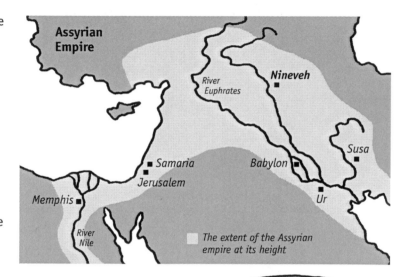

Assyrian Empire

Nineveh

River Euphrates

Susa

Samaria
Jerusalem
Babylon
Memphis
Ur

River Nile

The extent of the Assyrian empire at its height

So what about Nahum?

No one knows exactly when Nahum lived and prophesied. But it's likely that he was around in the 7th century BC when the empire was past its best and **falling apart**.

Nahum gleefully prophesies the **destruction of Nineveh**, the Assyrian capital city. His poetry is colorful and full of energy. Nineveh fell in 612 BC.

Nahum has inspired Jews and Christians living under evil regimes. **Tyrants** will be **overthrown** and God is a safe refuge for those who trust him.

Everyone who hears the news about you claps his hands at your fall, for who has not felt your endless cruelty?

Nahum's final words, spoken to Nineveh

HABAKKUK

Habakkuk is a sort of companion book to **Nahum**, because both prophets were tangling with the problem of the **aggressive superpowers** who dominated life at the time. For Nahum, it was the **Assyrians**. For Habakkuk (who probably lived later than Nahum) it was the **Babylonians**.

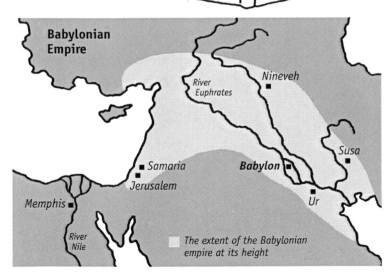

So it's another song of revenge then?

HABA KKUK

No. There's a **big difference** in tone between the two books. While Nahum dances on the Assyrians' grave, Habakkuk is close to **despair**. Although the **cruel** Assyrians are gone, they've been replaced by the even **crueller** Babylonians.

In the words of **The Who**, it's a case of...

"Meet the new boss. Same as the old boss..."

Habakkuk asks: how can **God** allow the violent Babylonians to **attack and destroy** people better than themselves? The answer he gets in chapter 2 is that God's judgment is on its way – **slowly**, but **inevitably**.

This promise restores Habakkuk's faith in God.

Babylonian Empire

River Euphrates

Nineveh

Susa

Samaria

Babylon

Jerusalem

Ur

Memphis

River Nile

The extent of the Babylonian empire at its height

ZEPHANIAH

Zephaniah, Zedekiah, Zechariah, Zaba... Zera... zzz... zzzzzz... zzz...

Judgment Day

Zephaniah's message was shocking. There was a popular belief at that time in **the Day of the Lord.** The Day of the Lord was the day when God would **save his people.** Their enemies would be crushed, Judah would rule the world, they'd all be fabulously rich, etc.

Zephaniah savagely turned this fantasy on its head. On the Day of the Lord, he said, it is **you, Judah,** who will be crushed. God will judge you for all your sins. He gives an awe-inspiring picture of **God's anger.** It gave rise to the whole idea of Judgment Day.

OK. Some orientation. Our man Zephaniah was a **fiery preacher** who prophesied in the reign of **King Josiah** (2 Chronicles 34–35) in the last 50 years before Judah was dragged off into exile.

Zephaniah looked around and he saw Judah sinking deeper and deeper into **violence** and the **worship of idols.** All this will bring down God's anger, he said.

**❝ The great day of the Lord
   is near...
it will be a day of fury,
a day of trouble and distress,
a day of ruin and destruction,
a day of darkness and gloom,
a black and cloudy day,
a day filled with the sound of
   war trumpets
and the battle-cry of
   soldiers... ❞**

The Day of the Lord in Zephaniah 1:14–16

HAGGAI

Haggai isn't on the A-list of Old Testament prophets. He isn't even on the B-list. We know **hardly anything** about him and his book is only two chapters long. What we do know is that he lived at the time when **the exiles** who returned from Babylon were trying to rebuild their lives in the **ruins of Jerusalem.**

A WAKE-UP CALL!

Haggai's book is a sharp reminder to the people who had resettled Jerusalem. They hadn't **rebuilt the Temple**, the focal point of their faith, even though they'd been back in the city for **16 years**. So why were they slacking?

■ **Opposition** – there was opposition from local people who complained to the emperor about the rebuilding (Ezra 4:1–5).

■ **Laziness** – the wealthy people of the city were busy looking after their own luxurious lifestyle (Haggai 1:3–4).

■ **Discouragement** – everyone knew the new temple would be nothing compared to Solomon's temple (Haggai 2:1–5).

Haggai was so successful in motivating the people to get building, that only four years later the Temple was completed. It stood for 500 years – longer than either the temples of Solomon or Herod.

Haggai goaded them into action. His message was: "Be strong and work!" And he gave them a promise too: "The glory of this present house will be greater than the glory of the former house" (Haggai 2:9).

ZECHARIAH

Zechariah is a curious book. It's in **two distinct halves**, which are very different from each other. Here's how the two halves of Zechariah look...

Visions in the night

Zechariah was in Jerusalem at the same time as **Haggai**, and the prophecies in chapters 1–8 were given when Haggai was active too. Zechariah has **eight visions** in the night, which include a **flying scroll** the size of a small aircraft, the **four riders** of the apocalypse and a woman in a **flying basket**. All of it is deeply symbolic and makes for a rather surreal read.

Oracles of the future

Chapters 9–14 don't have any strange visions, just "conventional" prophecy that seems to come from a much later time than chapters 1–8. They include two famous passages: the coming of the **Prince of Peace**, who rides on a **donkey** (Zechariah 9:9) and mourning over "the one they have **pierced**" (Zechariah 12:10). Both passages are quoted in the Gospels as referring to the life and death of Jesus.

So who wrote this book and why are its two halves so completely different from each other?

Part 1 was written with an optimistic message by a prophet named Zechariah who lived around 520 BC.

Part 2 was written much later (sometime after 332 BC) while the Jews were living under Greek domination. It was written by an unknown prophet, or a group of prophets.

THE BIBLE FROM SCRATCH

Malachi

Malachi is **the last** of the Old Testament prophets and he's the one who is closest in time to the New Testament. Like **Haggai** and **Zechariah**, who were around 70 years before him, Malachi prophesied to the people who had settled in Jerusalem **after the exile**. They were once again apathetic about their faith, saying, "It's useless to serve God."

Now where have I heard that before?

Oh... in Exodus, Numbers, Judges, 1 and 2 Kings, Isaiah, Amos, Hosea, etc... Lack of interest in God is one of the **long-playing themes** of the Bible.

Malachi also has a go at the **priests** for not doing their jobs seriously, **bosses** for cheating workers out of their wages and **husbands** for divorcing their wives. It was only when **Nehemiah** arrived on the scene, soon after Malachi's time, that these problems were put right.

Two passages in Malachi are full of **expectation** that God is about to do something **decisive**. Both of them are picked up by the writers of the New Testament...

> I will send my messenger to prepare the way for me.
>
> *Malachi 3:1 (see Mark 1:2)*

> But for you who revere my name, the sun of righteousness will rise with healing in its wings.
>
> *Malachi 4:2 (see Luke 1:78)*

Intro to the New Testament

In the early centuries of the church, Christians didn't trash the Old Testament scriptures in favor of the New Testament. Instead, they read them together, as one, seamless story of God's revelation to the human race.

Near the end of the Gospel of Mark (the earliest of the four Gospels, the accounts of Jesus' life) is a curious story. It comes right at the end of the arrest of Jesus in the middle of the night.

The spotlight of Mark's story has been on Jesus, as the soldiers grab him and Judas betrays him with a kiss, but suddenly the spotlight picks out a young man dressed only in a linen nightshirt at the back of the crowd. He's a follower of Jesus who maybe dashed from his bed to get to the scene in time. He isn't even named. The soldiers try to arrest him, but he slips away by shrugging off his nightshirt and fleeing naked.

The question is: why did Mark add this potentially comic moment in a scene of otherwise overwhelming tragedy? One theory is that Mark himself was the naked runner and that he put this story into his Gospel as a way of adding his signature to the whole production – rather like Alfred Hitchcock always appears in a walk-on, walk-off part in the first few minutes of his movies.

If the theory is true, then catching this glimpse of Mark on camera makes us remember that the 27 books which make up the New Testament were researched, assembled and written by real human beings. It also reminds us that they were living so close to the story, they were often in it themselves.

How did the New Testament come to be written? And what's inside it? The New Testament naturally falls into four sections, beginning with the four different accounts of Jesus' life known as the Gospels. These sections are...

- Jesus (Matthew to John)
- The Church (Acts)
- Letters (Romans to Jude)
- The End (Revelation)

All the books are written in Greek, and the most popular form of writing in the New Testament is letter-writing: 21 out of the 27 books are in fact letters. The others are stories (the Gospels and Acts) and a book of prophecy that is in a category all of its own (Revelation).

It's tempting to think that the four Gospels were the first books of the New Testament to be written, since they tell the story that kicked off the whole thing: the birth, life, death and resurrection of Jesus of Nazareth. And that the rest of the New Testament books followed after that. But it wasn't like that at all.

In the next few pages, we're going to speed through a reconstruction of how the New Testament was written. Biblical experts have argued – and still argue – over who wrote what when, so what follows is what most Catholic scholars believe.

In the beginning: Jesus

Let's start with something a bit obvious, but worth saying anyway: Jesus didn't write a book.

It wasn't that Jesus couldn't read or write, because in one of the stories about him he gives the reading in his local synagogue one Saturday, and the congregation comment afterwards on how good he was at doing it.

Most of the New Testament is the mail of the early church, with letters sent to communities of the first generation of Christians.

Ezra Pound's famous poem, 'Ballad of the Goodly Fere' (fere = mate or companion), imagines Simon the Zealot, one of Jesus' more rugged disciples, saying that Jesus was too much a man of action ever to have the patience to sit down with a pot of ink and parchment…

They'll no' get him a' in a book I think
Though they write it cunningly;
No mouse of the scrolls was the Goodly Fere
But aye loved the open sea.
Ezra Pound

Jesus didn't leave anything in writing, as far as we know. Instead, he was committed to speech and action. He spoke about the kingdom of God using parables, proverbs and sayings that were very "sticky" – they stuck in the memory of the people who heard them. He also did things – such as healing the sick, casting out demons and clashing with his religious enemies – which were dramatic and memorable, too.

This meant that after Jesus' death and resurrection, there were plenty of people around who remembered how he had acted and spoken, and had stories to pass on about him. Those stories, told at first by eyewitnesses and then retold over and over in the earliest Christian communities, were the initial ingredients that went into making the New Testament.

For an introduction to the parables of Jesus, see page 194.

While the New Testament is written in Greek, Jesus spoke in Aramaic, a dialect of Hebrew which some people have nicknamed Hebrew Lite. The decision of the New Testament writers to use Greek means that 99.9 per cent of the original words spoken by Jesus in Aramaic have been lost for ever. But intriguingly, just a handful of Aramaic words have slipped through into the earliest of the Gospels, Mark's. Maybe they were specially treasured by the first Christians as the actual words Jesus spoke in moments of crisis. The first two instances were commands spoken by Jesus at the climax of miracles of healing...

Talitha kumi!

Mark 5:41

"Little girl, arise" – these were the words Jesus used to raise a little girl who had died.

Ephphatha!

Mark 7:34

"Open up!" – Jesus gave this command to a deaf man, after putting his fingers into his ears.

The other original words of Jesus are preserved in the narrative of his arrest, suffering and death, and give us glimpses into his state of mind during the final crisis of his life...

Abba...

Mark 14:36

"Father" – this is the familiar, childlike word Jesus used for God when he prayed in the Garden of Gethsemane, just hours before his crucifixion.

Eloi, eloi, lama sabachthani!

Mark 15:34

"My God, my God, why have you forsaken me?" – these are the stark and desperate words Jesus cried out in his darkest moments on the cross.

Jesus died sometime around the year AD 30. During the next two decades, in the 30s and 40s, the sayings of Jesus and episodes from his life and death were being collected by the first Christian communities in Palestine. These stories and sayings were eventually taken up, first by Mark, then by Matthew and Luke, and finally by John, in writing their Gospels.

But that was decades in the future. Long before the Gospel writers got to work, something unexpected was happening.

The letters of Paul

One day in AD 50 in the city of Corinth, a man put his pen to a piece of parchment and started writing: "Paul, Silas and Timothy, to the church of the Thessalonians in God the Father and the Lord Jesus Christ: grace and peace to you." These are the opening words of what is probably the very first of all the New Testament books to be written, Paul's 1 Thessalonians.

After Jesus himself, the next biggest figure in the development of the New Testament is Paul, clocking up no fewer than 13 books (although his authorship of some of them is disputed). Paul was probably born sometime during AD 10–15, which made him 15 or 20 years younger than Jesus.

Paul's position in the New Testament is very curious. He wasn't one of the original 12 disciples; instead, he actively tried to murder the Christian faith in its cradle. But he was dramatically converted and became an ambitious and controversial pioneer, taking the good news about Jesus into what are now Turkey, Greece, Italy and possibly even Spain. He established churches in places that some of Jesus' original followers had probably never heard about.

154

"Lost" sayings of Jesus

Some sayings of Jesus never made it into the four Gospels. They have survived in other parts of the New Testament, in early Christian writings and in Islamic sources. Here's a small selection of these "lost" sayings which Jesus may have given...

It is more blessed to give than to receive.

Quoted by Paul in Acts 20:35

Repent, for it is better that a man find a cup of water in the age that is coming than all the riches of this world.

Coptic Apocryphal Gospel

The heavenly Father wills the repentance of the sinner, rather than his punishment.

Quoted by Justin Martyr

Split wood, I am there. Lift up a rock, you will find me there.

Gospel of Thomas

Better is a single footstep in my Father's house than all the wealth of this world.

Coptic Apocryphal Gospel

The world is a bridge: pass over it, but build no houses upon it.

Persian inscription on the gateway of the Great Mosque in Fatehpur Sikri, India

Whoever is near to me is near the fire. Whoever is far from me is far from the kingdom.

Gospel of Thomas

As Paul paced his room in Corinth, dictating his words to the Christians in Thessalonica to his amanuensis (that is, his secretary), the New Testament was finally being put down on paper – 20 years after the crucifixion.

Since Paul was the one who started writing up the new faith first, it's worth noticing a couple of innovative things he did which may have helped set the pace for everyone who came after him.

First, Paul wrote in Greek. He didn't write in Hebrew (the language of the Jewish faith and the Old Testament) or Aramaic (the language of Jesus and Palestine), but in Greek – the language of the Gentiles he had travelled so far to reach.

Lots of authors were writing in Greek in Paul's time. Greek was the international language of the day, used all over the Roman empire. Known as "common Greek", it was a much rougher version of the language than classical Greek, which had been used by philosophers such as Plato and Socrates over 300 years before Paul. But Paul's Greek was different even from the Greek used by the authors of his own time.

Experts used to puzzle over this. Why was Paul's Greek different? Was it because he was using some kind of Jewish-Greek dialect?

It was only when archaeologists began discovering ancient rubbish tips in Egypt, which were full of written bits and pieces that had been thrown out of homes, shops and offices in ancient times, that the problem was solved. The rubbish tips showed for the first time the sort of language people used when they were

It's an epistle from the apostle!

writing everyday, throwaway stuff: shopping lists, complaints to builders, letters home, receipts, children's notes. When these salvaged documents were compared with the letters of Paul and the other New Testament writings, it was obvious they were using the same kind of language.

It's clear now that Paul chose to write not in a polished, literary style, as any author with a reputation to maintain would do. Instead, he took the rough, everyday language of the streets and put it on paper. He wanted to communicate his message in words which were used in the market, the arena and the home – so that this new faith truly was a faith for everyone and every day.

Paul was a man for plain speaking...

For an introduction to the New Testament letters, see page 220.

> **When I came to you, brothers, I did not come with eloquence or superior wisdom as I proclaimed to you the testimony about God...**
>
> *1 Corinthians 2:1*

Second, Paul wrote letters. He didn't choose to give his teaching in the form of parables, or poetry, or abstract philosophy, as others in the Bible before him had done. Instead, he chose to write letters. The choice is interesting, because letters are intensely practical things. Paul's letters, like most people's, were written in the busyness and pressure of real life and in response to specific people and situations.

Some of his letters were written to fix a particular problem (Paul's letter to Philemon is about a fugitive slave – see page 247), while others were written in the heat of the moment.

The Church at Corinth
Depravity Street
CORINTH, Ancient Greece

The most dramatic example of a "heat of the moment" letter is 1 Corinthians, which was flame-grilled and sent to Christians who had got themselves into deep trouble over food, sex and quarrelling – see page 226 for more details, or better still, read the letter itself.

Despite all that, Paul's letters aren't simply filled with problem-solving. He wrote passages of incredible power and beauty, such as his meditation on love (1 Corinthians 13), and pages of closely argued theology, such as his teaching on how the death of Jesus is God's response to human sin (Romans 3–8).

Paul's letters were written in the 50's and early 60's. They're arranged in descending order of length (just like the prophets in the Old Testament), and with Paul's most personal letters at the end of the collection. So if you want to let yourself into Paul's writings gently, read them in reverse order.

Mark, the first Gospel

The AD 60s, 30 years after the crucifixion, was a fiery decade for the young Christian faith. In the summer of AD 64 the great fire of Rome broke out and raged for nine days, destroying 10 out of the 14 districts of the city.

The homeless population was convinced the fire must have been started by someone, and when the finger of blame started to point towards Nero, an unpopular and unhinged emperor, Nero in turn pointed to the Christians of Rome. This triggered the first-ever wave of persecution against Christians.

The Roman historian Tacitus, who was a young boy at the time, later described the cruelties inflicted on Christians (turn over to page 160)...

The alternative
New Testament

*The New Testament hasn't always been
arranged in the same order of books as we have
it now. In the early centuries of the church, it
was usually arranged in four sections and was
produced as four separate volumes...*

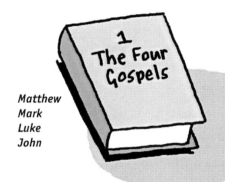

Acts
James
1 Peter
2 Peter
1 John
2 John
3 John
Jude

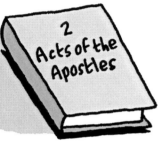

*Matthew
Mark
Luke
John*

*Acts was grouped with seven of the
non-Paul letters to make a book of its own.
Some have argued the letters were ordered
this way as the letters of James to Jude
represent the preaching of the gospel to
the Jews, while Paul's letters represent the
preaching of the gospel to the Gentiles.*

*Romans
1 Corinthians
2 Corinthians
Galatians
Ephesians
Philippians
Colossians
1 Thessalonians
2 Thessalonians
Hebrews
1 Timothy
2 Timothy
Titus
Philemon*

*Hebrews was included among the
letters of Paul, as the early church
believed (wrongly) that Paul was its
author.*

Revelation

Mockery of every sort was added to their deaths. Covered with the skins of beasts, they were torn by dogs and perished, or were nailed to crosses, or were doomed to the flames and burned, to serve as a nightly illumination when daylight had expired. Nero offered his gardens for the spectacle...
Tacitus

The Roman persecution of AD 64–65 is said to have claimed the lives of Peter and Paul, the two leaders of the first generation of Christians. Tradition tells us Peter was crucified, while Paul was beheaded by the sword.

It also set a terrible precedent: from this point on, if the Roman authorities in cities around the empire wanted to make an example of someone, or the mobs were looking for scapegoats, the Christians were easy prey. The threat and reality of persecution colors many of the later books in the New Testament.

A second great blow fell in AD 70, when the Roman general Titus crushed a Jewish revolt against Roman rule by besieging Jerusalem and destroying the temple which Herod had built and Jesus had known. He left Jerusalem in ruins.

For an introduction to the Gospels, see page 174.

Sometime in the five years between these two events – the fire of Rome and the fall of Jerusalem – Mark's Gospel was written, according to a good number of experts. This was an important moment, as Mark was the first person to put down on paper an account of the life of Jesus. Until this time, the only writings the Christians had possessed were the letters of Paul and others.

Apart from the naked sprint in chapter 14 of his Gospel, some experts believe Mark also appears in the book of Acts, where he's called John Mark (Acts 12:12). His mom kept a house in

Jerusalem where the first Christians met to pray. Possibly this was the upper room where Jesus and the disciples ate the Last Supper. Later, Mark became a much-valued assistant and companion of Peter, and maybe this is how he found out enough about Jesus to write his Gospel.

The situation was probably something like this: while Paul was trotting round the Roman empire founding and visiting Gentile Christian communities, Peter was doing something similar for the Jewish Christian communities, with Mark alongside him. Peter ended up preaching in Rome, telling his stories about all that Jesus said and did, and Mark was there as his interpreter, translating the preaching into Latin, perhaps. As Mark sat there, hearing again and again Peter's stories, he started to write them down. And so the first Gospel began to be written.

Some experts believe that Mark only started writing his Gospel once Peter had died. This is because Mark's Gospel includes details about Peter that would have been very embarrassing to publish if Peter had still been alive – such as the way Peter denied knowing Jesus to save his skin after Jesus had been arrested.

Mark's Gospel is the shortest and most action-packed of the four Gospels. The very first verse tells us why Mark is writing: "This is the Good News about Jesus Christ, the Son of God." There's no mucking about. From there on, he plunges straight in, introducing John the Baptist in the very next sentence. He's not interested in long accounts of Jesus' birth, as Matthew and Luke are. Instead, he sets off like a rocket, so that just 16 verses in, Jesus is already calling the first disciples.

Mark portrays Jesus as a man of power and action, who had come into the world to attack and triumph over the forces of evil.

The ending of Mark's Gospel is one of the great puzzles of the New Testament. Mark's story seems to be cut short, with the women standing outside the empty tomb of Jesus. It ends with the words, "they were afraid". Some experts say Mark's last page or two must have been lost, while others think he meant to end where he did.

Matthew and Luke both used Mark in writing their Gospels, and then added material unique to each of them.

Jesus is sharply human in Mark, maybe because we're seeing him through the eyes of Peter.

The stories about Jesus are rough and ready, and they have immediacy, color and impact. We see Jesus doing miracles in a very physical way: putting his fingers in a deaf man's ears; spitting in the mud and making a paste to put on a blind man's eyes. One of his miracles doesn't work quite right and Jesus has to have a second go at it. This kind of thing never happens in the more sophisticated Gospels of Matthew and Luke!

As the earliest Gospel, Mark is very direct about Jesus. At times he seems immediately close. This was the experience of Anthony Bloom, an atheist surgeon who worked with the French resistance during the Second World War and who later became head of the Russian Orthodox Church in Britain. His experience of reading Mark started him on the road to faith...

I counted the chapters of the four Gospels to be sure I read the shortest... I started to read St Mark's Gospel. While I was reading the beginning of St Mark's Gospel, before I reached the third chapter, I suddenly became aware that on the other side of my desk there was a presence. And the certainty was so strong that it was Christ standing there that it has never left me.
Metropolitan Anthony

Matthew, Luke and Acts

The 70s, 80s and 90s of the first century AD saw the biggest period of writing of the New Testament, and it's likely that Matthew and Luke led the field. Each of them used the Gospel of Mark as a major source for their writing, but they had other documents to work from, too, and they wrote for different audiences: Matthew wrote for Jewish Christians living in Palestine, while Luke wrote for Gentiles. Matthew presents Jesus as the fulfilment of the Old Testament and this is his unique approach among the four Gospels.

For example, take the story of Jesus riding into Jerusalem on the back of a donkey, a few days before his death. While Luke simply tells the story, Matthew shows how the words of the prophet Zechariah, written hundreds of years earlier, are coming to life in this event. And so he adds these words to the story...

> **This happened in order to make what the prophet had said come true: "Tell the city of Zion, look, your king is coming to you! He is humble, and rides on a donkey."**

Matthew 21:4–5

Matthew follows this approach again and again, picking up verses from the Old Testament prophecies and sticking them on to incidents in the life of Jesus – sometimes in ways which seem rather odd to us now. You can sense his excitement as he hears the powerful echoes of the Old Testament in what Jesus said and did. The murder of Bethlehem's children, Jesus growing up in Nazareth, Jesus teaching in parables – for Matthew, these details had been forecast centuries earlier and they authenticated Jesus' mission. You can see how Matthew matches individual prophecies to the life of Jesus on page 176.

The second way Matthew links with the Old Testament is by casting Jesus in the role of Moses II. Jesus is a bigger and better Moses. Just as Moses went up Mt Sinai to receive the Ten

The wise men... they're only in Matthew's Gospel.

For an introduction to Matthew, see page 176.

Commandments from God, so in Matthew chapters 5–7, Jesus goes up a hill in Galilee and preaches the Sermon on the Mount. In it, he explicitly takes the Law of Moses and contradicts it, replacing it with something better...

You have heard that it was said, "An eye for an eye, and a tooth for a tooth." But now I tell you: do not take revenge on someone who wrongs you. If anyone slaps you on the right cheek, let him slap your left cheek too.

Matthew 5:38–39

Jesus is doing something new with the Law of Moses. He's changing it, stretching it, deepening it, fulfilling it. He has come to bring a new agreement, a new testament, between God and the people. This is how Matthew commends the life and teaching of Jesus to his Jewish readers. And for us, his book is like glue which holds the Old and New Testaments firmly together, showing that the same God works in both.

Meanwhile, Luke was writing a very different book for a very different audience. His book is in two parts (Luke plus Acts) and takes up one-quarter of the New Testament, making Luke the most prolific Christian writer of his time. Luke-Acts would have covered 64 ft (or 20 m) of scroll, which was a lot of scroll even in those days.

So who was this blockbusting author? Luke was a very common name in the Roman world, but from the earliest days of the church it was believed that the particular Luke who wrote Luke-Acts was none other than Dr. Luke, who travelled with Paul on some of his journeys around the Mediterranean.

Luke is probably the most popular of the four Gospels today, and it's because his picture of Jesus is so warm and human. Luke draws out the love and compassion of Jesus for ordinary people. He wants to communicate how Jesus drove a truck through the social conventions of his time. How he had time for people who were poor or had been left out of the community. How he said it was easier for a camel to go through the eye of a needle than for a rich man to enter the kingdom of God.

That's why Luke records events where Jesus healed (or simply accepted) disadvantaged people. Or where he told a parable about them. There's the parable of the Good Samaritan, about people who were hated in Jesus' day because of their race. There's the parable of the Pharisee and the taxman – there's another hated group: the taxmen. Some things don't change across the centuries! There's the story of Jesus reaching out to touch a leper.

Luke also spotlights Jesus' attitude towards women. The gulf between men and women was incredibly wide at that time. Women weren't taught to read – they were considered too inferior. They weren't allowed to testify in court, because their talk was considered totally unreliable. In contrast, Luke shows us Jesus relating to women. In the story of Mary and Martha, Martha breaks off from doing the dishes to get mad at Jesus. Why has he allowed Mary to sit in with the men to hear his teaching? Jesus responds...

For more on Luke's Gospel, see page 190.

> **Martha, Martha, you are worried and upset about many things, but only one thing is needed. Mary has chosen what is better, and it will not be taken away from her.**

Luke 10:41–42

Another valuable thing Luke does is connect up the life of Jesus with the mission of his first followers. Luke's 64 ft scroll starts off in Jerusalem, with the parents of John the Baptist, but ends up in Rome, with Paul waiting to go on trial for his life before the emperor. When you think of it, this is amazingly helpful, because Luke-Acts bridges the world of the Gospels and the world of the New Testament letters, and they are two very different worlds.

The Gospels are full of Jewish details: parables, synagogues, Pharisees, figs, fishing towns, vineyards, village weddings, the Sea of Galilee. The world of Jesus is basically rural. But when you look at the letters of Paul, you're in a completely different world. The letters are full of Roman details: running the race, winning the crown, refusing to worship idols, obeying the emperor, putting on "the armour of God". The world of Paul is basically urban.

The stepping stone between the rural, Jewish world of the Gospels and the urban, Roman world of the letters is Luke-Acts, which carries us across from one to the other by including them in one continuous story.

THE BIBLE FROM SCRATCH

Sadly, Luke and Acts were separated in the 2nd century AD, when someone had the bright idea of putting the Gospel of John between them. But it's well worth reading them as one book, just as Dr. Luke intended.

The back end of the New Testament

No one is sure how it happened, but sometime between the 70s and 90s of the first century, the letters of Paul to individual churches around the Mediterranean world started to collect together, like little rivers flowing into a big lake. Some experts believe it was the publication of Luke's book of Acts which did it: suddenly, the story of Paul's pioneering work became known for the first time, Paul became a celebrity and spiritual hero and everyone wanted to read what he had written.

Paul's letters had probably been copied and passed around among local churches ever since the time he wrote them. In fact, one letter describes this happening...

> **After this letter has been read to you, see that it is also read in the church of the Laodiceans and that you in turn read the letter from Laodicea.**

Colossians 4:16

But now his letters were copied on a big scale and collections of them were probably available in Corinth, Ephesus, Rome and the other urban centres of the new faith. By the beginning of the 90s, other writers started to quote from Paul as if his letters were widely known and available to read. The letter of 2 Peter certainly knows about a collection of his letters...

> **Paul writes the same way in all his letters...**

2 Peter 3:16

Meanwhile, as the first century drew to a close, the books which eventually lodged at the back of the New Testament were probably being written: James, Jude, the three letters of John and the book of Revelation.

Revelation is one of the most bizarre books of the Bible. Parts of it read like a drug trip gone badly wrong – with its visions of creatures with multiple heads, people dipping their robes in blood or being cast into a lake of fire – and it has even been dismissed as the product of a sick mind. But the sickness suffered by John was caught from the terrible times in which he lived.

John was in crisis – he was desperate to know why the world was going so badly wrong and why God was doing nothing to stop it. Christians were facing violent persecution under the Emperor Domitian (AD 81–96), who was unusual among emperors in declaring himself to be a god *before* he died. While other New Testament writers called for Christians to stand firm under fire, John wanted answers to his questions: where was God, and what was he doing about the suffering of his people?

It's no good... I don't understand eschatology!

Don't worry. It's not the end of the world.

When people are under extreme pressure, strange things happen. In the book of Revelation, the scenery is torn open and John sees what is happening backstage, in heaven. He sees angels hurrying to do their work, and hears the voices and songs of heaven, and sees the titanic battles between the forces of good and evil. All the ambiguities of human life are dissolved as John sees directly what is happening behind the scenes. By the end of his book, he comes to understand that evil will be crushed and the purposes of God will finally triumph.

Unfortunately, some people approach the book of Revelation as if it were a code waiting to be cracked, or a detailed timetable to the end of the world. But if instead of obsessing over the details you look at the bigger picture in this book, its images of global destruction and the promise of the future kingdom of God are themes which speak powerfully today.

Desmond Tutu, Archbishop of Cape Town during South Africa's apartheid era, used to encourage people during their fight against injustice by pointing them to the book of Revelation...

Don't give up! Don't get discouraged! I have read the end of the book! We win!
Desmond Tutu

The book of Revelation has a colorful cast, including the Whore of Babylon, the Beast, Satan, and the four riders of the Apocalypse (pictured above).

John's Gospel

When was the New Testament finished? When did the last writer lay down his pen? It used to be argued that John's Gospel was completed close to the year 200, until a tiny fragment of papyrus with words from John chapter 18 written on it was discovered in Egypt and dated to about 125. Experts now believe John's Gospel was completed sometime between the years 80 and 100 (while the second letter of Peter was probably written in the year 130).

The trad view is that the Gospel was written by John, the disciple of Jesus. John would need to have lived to a ripe old age to write his Gospel some 60 years after the crucifixion, but legend claims he did live into his 80s, and that he was a lively enough old chap to leap out of a public bath when a notorious heretic took to the waters beside him!

John is very different from Matthew, Mark and Luke, which are known as the synoptic Gospels. "Synoptic" means "single eye", and it's true that these three books share a similar way of looking at Jesus and telling his story. Meanwhile, John's gaze is unique.

For a start, he leaves out all of Jesus' most famous parables and he includes only seven of Jesus' many miracles. In their place, he shows Jesus having long conversations with people who never even appear in Matthew, Mark or Luke – people such as Nicodemus ("You must be born again!" Jesus tells him), or the Samaritan woman Jesus meets at a well. John also includes long passages of teaching from Jesus which are different from anything you'll find in the synoptic Gospels.

Despite the puzzle over why John is so at odds with Matthew, Mark and Luke, his Gospel has always been deeply loved and treasured by Christians. John alone tells us that Jesus is "the Word made flesh" (John 1:14) and that "God so loved the world that he gave his one and only Son" (John 3:16). Love, life and light are big themes in John, and Jesus also speaks openly about "the Father" and his relationship with him.

Out of all the New Testament writers, John and Paul set the agenda for the way Jesus was to be understood for the next 2,000 years. Our understanding of Jesus as God living as a human being on earth, and as the one who redeems us from the penalty of sin, comes from John and Paul. John's role in doing this was understood from early on…

No one has dared to give so pure a revelation of the divinity as John. We must make bold to say the Gospels are the fulfilment of the whole Bible and John's Gospel is the fulfilment of the Gospels.
Origen, 3rd century

With the completion of John, the church had no fewer than four accounts of Jesus to choose from in selecting its "official" life of Christ. But instead of holding a sort of beauty contest to see which Gospel it liked best, the church decided it wanted all four. Which is how the New Testament ended up including Matthew, Mark, Luke and John.

Having more than one Gospel has advantages, of course, because each writer includes stories and sayings the others have left out. But it also has disadvantages, because as soon as you allow more than one version of Jesus' life, you invite people to spot the discrepancies between them and you raise the whole question of how accurately we can know about Jesus anyway. Over the centuries, the various enemies of Christianity have hugely enjoyed this "weakness" in the Christian scriptures.

Discomfort over having three too many Gospels was felt as early as the 2nd century AD, because a book called *The Diatessaron* was produced, which blended the four Gospels into one neat account. For several centuries, it replaced the four Gospels in some churches. In more recent times, people have tried to produce harmonies of the Gospels. But the fact is that Matthew, Mark and Luke often sing discordantly, while John... well... John is singing a different melody altogether.

Irenaeus, Bishop of Lyons at the end of the 2nd century, spoke of there being just one gospel – one message of good news – in four different forms. He said that just as there are four points of the compass, and four winds, and four creatures in the book of Revelation (Revelation 4:7, which echoes Ezekiel 1:10), so there must be four Gospels, no more and no less.

This, by the way, is where the symbols of the four evangelists came from (shown on the right). The four living creatures of

Since the 2nd century AD, the four Gospels have been symbolized by a man (Matthew), lion (Mark), ox (Luke) and eagle (John). They're taken from Ezekiel's vision in Ezekiel 1:10.

Revelation 4:7 were applied after the time of Irenaeus to the four Gospels: the lion for Mark, the ox for Luke, the man for Matthew and the eagle for John.

Irenaeus basically settled the question of "how many Gospels?" for the church. Since then, most other leaders in the church have been happy to talk about the distinctive approaches of the four Gospels. For example...

Matthew wrote for the Hebrews
  the wonderful works of Christ,
And Mark for Italy, Luke for Greece,
John, the great preacher, for all,
  walking in heaven.
Gregory of Nazianzus, 4th century

If you prefer your faith to be all sewn up and consistent, with God very much the boss, then having four Gospels which sometimes disagree with each other is probably going to feel a bit untidy and uncomfortable. But if you're happy with a faith that is frayed at the edges and has unanswered questions, with our messy, fallible humanity very much in the picture, then you'll probably enjoy the four different pictures painted by the Gospel writers.

Despite having four different angles on his life, Jesus remains elusive and is not captured on the page. He is the living – and not the inky – Word of God.

JESUS

Here are **four small books** which changed the world. They tell the story of a **carpenter** from an obscure village in northern Israel who became a **teacher, healer and miracle-worker** and was put to death by the authorities when his message became too controversial. They tell the story of **Jesus**.

Mark – this is the shortest of these four books, and shows Jesus as a man of strong emotions and decisive action

Matthew – shows Jesus as a great teacher, with his feet planted firmly in the Old Testament, as a sort of "second Moses"

John – is very different from Matthew, Mark and Luke, zooming in on the essential meaning of Jesus' life and death, with sayings of Jesus found nowhere else

Luke – emphasizes Jesus' revolutionary focus on disadvantaged people: the poor, women, outcasts, people living on the edges of society

INTRO

This section of the Bible focuses on a **single person.** It records the **birth, life, death** and **resurrection** of Jesus, who started out as an ordinary man in an ordinary town, but ended his life as an **inspiring** and **controversial teacher.** The books in this section raise the question...

Who was Jesus?

We'll come back to this question later...

The story of Jesus is told in **Matthew, Mark, Luke** and **John**, which are known as the four **Gospels.** "Gospel" is an old English word meaning **good news**, and that's how these books describe themselves. Each of them is a "life of Jesus".

It took a while for the first Christians to collect the stories about Jesus and get his life **down in writing.** Before that time, you would have to go and hear someone like Peter talking about what Jesus said and did to find out about him.

According to ancient tradition, Peter's stories about Jesus were written down by Mark and put into his Gospel. See page 179.

See page 179.

GOSPEL HITS

For a quick intro to what the Gospels are like, take a look at these stories from the life of Jesus...

1 Jesus works a miracle
Mark 4:37–41

2 Jesus tells a parable
Luke 15:11–32

3 Jesus heals someone
Luke 18:35–43

4 Jesus feeds the hungry
Matthew 14:15–21

5 Jesus teaches people
Matthew 6:24–34

6 Jesus shows compassion
John 8:2–11

Three of the Gospels are **very different** from the other one...

SYNOPTIC GOSPELS

Matthew, Mark and Luke are all books in the same "family" – they're similar in **the stories** they include, the way they **tell** those stories, and in the way they (mostly) agree about the **order of events.**

In these Gospels, **Jesus is cautious** when it comes to talking about who he is.

JOHN'S GOSPEL

John's Gospel feels as if it comes from a different family. John tells **different stories** from the ones told by Matthew, Mark and Luke. Also, Jesus doesn't speak in parables, but gives **long speeches** and **talks openly** about his identity as God's Son.

Because of this, experts say John is an **interpretation** of Jesus' life, and not a straight retelling of his story.

So when were they written?

Mark's Gospel was probably the **first to be written**, sometime before the year AD 70, about 40 years after Jesus died.

At the other end of the scale, John's Gospel was probably the **last to be written.** The oldest scrap of any Gospel ever discovered (from John, pictured below) is from about AD 125, so John must have been written before that time.

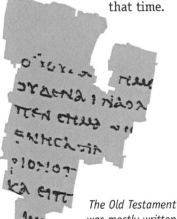

The Old Testament was mostly written in Hebrew, but the New Testament is in Greek.

matthew

Matthew's Gospel is the **first book** in the New Testament, and so it's nearest (page-wise) to the **Old Testament.** That's appropriate, because Matthew, more than Mark, Luke or John, shows that Jesus is **the fulfilment** of the Old Testament hope for a **messiah** (See page 185). Matthew partly wrote to show his Jewish readers that faith in Jesus was natural, as Jesus' life and teaching sprang from deep **Jewish roots.**

OK. So how does he do it?

First, Matthew keeps quoting passages from the Old Testament **prophets and psalms**, and then saying how the life and teaching of Jesus fits them **like a glove.** Here's a typical example which comes after Jesus has been **healing** sick people...

This was to fulfil what was spoken through the prophet Isaiah: "He took up our infirmities and carried our disease." Matthew 8:17

MATTHEW 1:23
JESUS IS IMMANUEL – "GOD WITH US"

MATTHEW 4:15-16
JESUS PREACHES IN GALILEE

MATTHEW 13:35
WHY JESUS USED PARABLES

MATTHEW 2:18
THE KILLING OF BETHLEHEM'S CHILDREN

MATTHEW 21:5
JESUS ENTERS JERUSALEM RIDING ON A DONKEY

MATTHEW 12:18-20
JESUS AS GOD'S SERVANT

MATTHEW 2:23
JESUS IS TO BE BROUGHT UP IN NAZARETH

MATTHEW 27:9-10
HOW JUDAS'S BLOOD MONEY WAS SPENT

On the left are some other examples. The point Matthew's making is that the God of Israel was alive and active in Jesus' life. Jesus echoes and fulfils the Old Testament.

THE BIBLE FROM SCRATCH

2 Second, Matthew seems to cast Jesus in the role of **Moses**, the great lawgiver of the Old Testament, as if Jesus was **Moses II**. Matthew sees Jesus as having the same sort of incredible impact that Moses had on God's people in the past.

Here's Jesus bringing the "new law" – a way of life which fulfils and deepens the Law of Moses...

> You have heard that it was said: "Love your neighbour and hate your enemy." But I tell you: 'Love your enemies and pray for those who persecute you.

Matthew 5:43–44

Matthew paints a striking picture of Jesus as the **great teacher**, telling the people, with amazing power, what **the real meaning** of the Old Testament Law is.

MATTHEW: ONE-TIME FAVORITE GOSPEL

In the **first centuries** of the church, Matthew was everyone's **favorite Gospel**. While John and Luke are very popular today, Matthew was the big read back then. This is probably why it was placed **first in the list** of the four Gospels.

Here's why...

Matthew collected a huge amount of the teaching of Jesus and arranged it in easy-to-follow themes: the kingdom of God, discipleship and so on.

Matthew contains almost all the teaching of Jesus that you can find in both Mark and Luke... so it's a one-stop read.

MATTHEW'S GOSPEL

The Gospel includes plenty of practical material for individual Christians and churches, with teaching on how Christians should behave. Take a look at the Sermon on the Mount (Matthew 5–7) and you can see that Matthew's Gospel was deservedly popular.

Despite its Jewish themes, Matthew is very strong on the worldwide mission of the church. It is big on encouragement to spread the faith...

> Go and make disciples of all nations...

Jesus, in Matthew 28:19

the Twelve

Like many **Jewish rabbis**, Jesus gathered a group of disciples around him, which included some **70 people**. But the disciples who were closest to him are known as **The Twelve**, and they spent a lot of time **travelling** with Jesus and listening to his teaching. Here they are...

Simon Peter – with James and John, he was closest to Jesus. His faith was strong, but he could be rash and hot-headed. See page 214.

Judas Iscariot – he betrayed Jesus to his enemies. After Jesus died, he committed suicide. See page 206.

Andrew – Peter's brother. Both of them were fishermen.

James (son of Alphaeus) – nothing is known about him.

John – he was the closest of all to Jesus. For more on James and John, see page 184.

Bartholomew, also known as Nathanael.

Disciples

You can read the famous story of how Jesus **called** the **first disciples** (Simon and Andrew, plus James and John) in Mark 1:14-20. Jesus called them for a reason...

❝ ... that they **might be with him** and that **he might send them** out to **preach** and to **have authority** to **drive** out demons. **❞**

Mark 3:14-15

James – brother of John. They were both fishermen.

Thomas – famous for asking awkward questions about the resurrection.

Philip – came from Galilee. He asked lots of questions about who Jesus was.

Matthew – a taxman who left his well-paid job to follow Jesus. Also known as Levi.

Judas (son of James) – also known as Thaddaeus.

Simon (the Zealot) – before meeting Jesus he was probably part of a group of terrorists taking action against the Romans.

Apologies to Leonardo

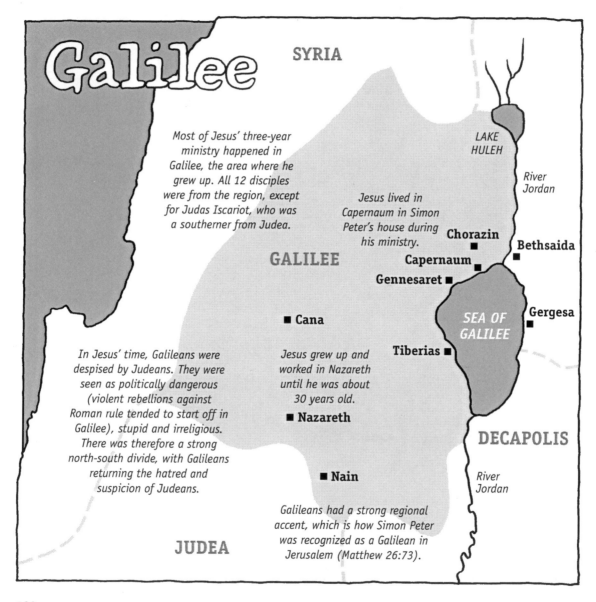

Galilee

SYRIA

Most of Jesus' three-year ministry happened in Galilee, the area where he grew up. All 12 disciples were from the region, except for Judas Iscariot, who was a southerner from Judea.

Jesus lived in Capernaum in Simon Peter's house during his ministry.

GALILEE

LAKE HULEH

River Jordan

■ Chorazin

■ Bethsaida

■ Capernaum

Gennesaret ■

■ Cana

SEA OF GALILEE

■ Gergesa

Tiberias ■

In Jesus' time, Galileans were despised by Judeans. They were seen as politically dangerous (violent rebellions against Roman rule tended to start off in Galilee), stupid and irreligious. There was therefore a strong north-south divide, with Galileans returning the hatred and suspicion of Judeans.

Jesus grew up and worked in Nazareth until he was about 30 years old.

■ Nazareth

DECAPOLIS

River Jordan

■ Nain

Galileans had a strong regional accent, which is how Simon Peter was recognized as a Galilean in Jerusalem (Matthew 26:73).

JUDEA

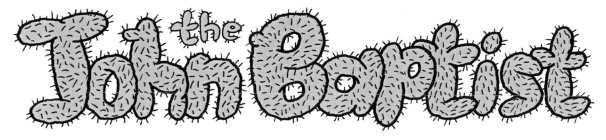

John the Baptist

John the Baptist – he was a Lutheran, right?

Duh.

John the Baptist appears right at **the beginning** of the story of Jesus' three-year ministry. He was a **fiery prophet** and is an important person in the Bible's scheme of things. He even gets his own **trailer** in the Old Testament – the book of Malachi (see page 147), written some 400 years pre-Jesus, said that before the coming of **the Messiah**, a prophet like Elijah would appear to prepare the way for him...

"I will send you the prophet Elijah"

Jesus identified John as this prophet (Matthew 11:14). He also said that John was **the greatest** of all Israel's prophets (Luke 7:18–35).

REPENT!

This was John's basic message. "Repent" is a word that means: "Stop sinning! Turn back to God!"

John lived in the desert and ate a diet of **locusts** and **wild honey** (Mark 1:4–6).

He baptized people in the **River Jordan** as a sign that their sins were forgiven, and he also baptized **Jesus** (Matthew 3:13–17).

Later, John had **doubts** about whether Jesus really was the Son of God (Luke 7:18–23)

When John attacked the corruption of **Herod Antipas,** he was thrown into prison and **killed** (Matthew 14:1–12).

MARK

It's the shortest of the four accounts of Jesus' life...

and the most gripping...

Mark probably wrote before Matthew, Luke or John, which makes his account the first...

Mark doesn't bother telling us about the birth of Jesus, but jumps straight in at his baptism and the call of the disciples...

Mark is interested in showing us both the human and the divine sides of Jesus.

Those are the headlines... now read on...

Mark's **in a hurry** to tell his story. His book is full of action, and Mark keeps the events coming so thick and fast they almost tread on each others' toes. One of his favourite words is **immediately**, as he shows Jesus moving **quickly** and **decisively** from event to event.

For example...

Immediately he was cured... **immediately** Jesus knew what they were thinking... **immediately** the girl stood up and walked around... **immediately** Jesus made his disciples get into the boat... **immediately** the demon threw the boy to the ground... **immediately** he received his sight and followed Jesus along the road... etc...

WHO WROTE IT?

There's good evidence that the book was written by **John Mark**, a follower of Jesus who became **Peter's assistant** when Peter was in Rome.

If that evidence is right, then Mark's Gospel is probably full of stories told to Mark by **Peter** himself – or which Mark picked up by listening to **Peter's preaching**.

That makes sense, because a lot of the stories in Mark sound like eyewitness accounts... they have lots of vivid, eyewitnessy details.

And also, if they're Peter's stories, you'd expect them to be like Peter himself – a bit blunt, and to the point. Which is just how Mark's Gospel is.

*Mark's Gospel spotlights two important aspects of the **identity** of Jesus...*

Human being

Mark shows us the human Jesus. Jesus so **heavily asleep** through exhaustion that even a storm doesn't wake him up (Mark 4:35–41). Jesus **getting angry** with his disciples for being a bit thick about what he was trying to teach them (Mark 8:14–21). Jesus **feeling alone and anguished** just before his arrest, returning to the disciples again and again for human company, only to find them asleep (Mark 14:32–42).

Son of God

Mark also shows us Jesus as the Son of God. Mark is an Eastern book, and in Eastern books, authors used the **beginning**, **middle** and **end** as key places to plant clues about the meaning of the whole book. In these three key places in Mark, Jesus is audibly declared to be **the Son of God**.

This happens at his **baptism** (Mark 1:11)... at his **transfiguration** (Mark 9:7)... and at his **crucifixion** (Mark 15:39).

It's as if Mark is saying to his readers...

Look! This Jesus was God's own Son. Follow him!

James&John

James and John were **two brothers** who ran their family's **fishing business** – until Jesus met them and called them to become his disciples. Jesus nicknamed them the **sons of thunder**.

A bit electrifying, were they?

Two incidents tell us about the **fiery character** of James and John. In Mark 10:35–45 they asked Jesus for **the best places** in his kingdom. And in Luke 9:51–56 they wanted to call down **fire from heaven** on a village that wouldn't welcome Jesus. They were volatile!

THE THREE

Despite their hot temperaments (or perhaps because of them), **James** and **John**, plus **Peter**, were the closest people to Jesus. At three **important moments**, this group of three disciples plays a key part...

- **Mark 5:35–43** – Jesus raises Jairus's daughter.
- **Mark 9:2–9** – Jesus is transfigured.
- **Mark 14:32–42** – Jesus prays before his death.

James

Out of Peter, James and John, James was **third in closeness** to Jesus. We know a lot less about him than we do about John or Peter.

In Acts 12:2, James was "**put to death** by the sword" by king Herod Agrippa I. This happened about 14 years after Jesus' death.

John

John was the **closest of all** to Jesus. He's identified as the cryptically-named "disciple whom Jesus loved" in John's Gospel. John and Peter led the **Jerusalem church** (see Acts 3–4), and the trad view is that he wrote **John's Gospel**, the **letters of John** and the book of **Revelation**.

MESSIAH

"Messiah" is a Hebrew word. The Greek version of it is "Christ". Both of these words mean "a person who has been anointed by God." In the Old Testament, it was kings who were anointed with oil to show that the power of God was upon them.

David was Israel's greatest king. But he was followed by a line of **weak or evil** rulers who brought the nation to disaster. So the Jewish people began to hope for a sort of **super-king**, the messiah, who would be sent by God at the end of time to **save them** from their enemies and **rule them** for ever with justice. This became a powerful symbol of hope that one day everything would be put right.

Here's how the **Old Testament** saw the messiah...

Isaiah 9:2-7
The Prince of Peace

Isaiah 11:1-9
The messiah's reign

Ezekiel 37:24-25
A king like David to rule for ever

Psalm 2
The scourge of the nations

Up to the time of Jesus, Israel was ruled harshly by the **Greeks** and then by the **Romans**. The Jewish people now saw the coming messiah as a **warrior-king** who would destroy Israel's military oppressors.

This is why Jesus was **very cautious** in his own lifetime about allowing others to call him "messiah". But his followers proclaimed that he was **descended from David** (for example, Matthew 1:1) and that he was Israel's true messiah. This is why he is still known as Jesus **Christ**.

That's what he'll do to the Greeks!

miracles

If you open Matthew, Mark or Luke at almost any page, you can't help finding the story of **a miracle** Jesus did. He brought sight to blind people, turned water into wine, calmed a storm and healed illnesses.

> But do we have to believe in Jesus' miracles? Why not just dump them and focus on Jesus as a great teacher?

Because it's impossible to cut out of the Gospels the miracles of Jesus without leaving them in **shreds**! Almost **one-third** of Mark's Gospel deals with miracles done by Jesus. The miracles were **central** to his life.

> But there were lots of so-called miracle workers around in Jesus' time. It was nothing so special!

Yes, there were many "miracle workers" around then. But Jesus' miracles were **very different**. He didn't use magical words or actions. His miracles were motivated by his **love** for people or to point them to **God**. And Jesus was no great showman or entertainer, wanting to draw a crowd to see his impressive tricks. Instead, he often told people to **keep quiet** about what they had seen him do (see Mark 5:43).

So **why** did Jesus do miracles anyway?

In the first three Gospels, the word used for **miracle** is **act of power**. Jesus had come to confront the powers of evil that had damaged the world God had made. This damage could be seen in **illnesses**, people possessed by **occult powers**, and ultimately in **death** itself. Jesus' miracles were mighty acts which healed the damage – they were the **kingdom of God** engaging with the kingdom of evil.

John's Gospel is different. John records only seven miracles of Jesus, and unlike Matthew, Mark and Luke, the word he uses for them is **signs**. Here Jesus' miracles don't only show God's kingdom has arrived in power, but that the **king himself** has come – in the person of Jesus. The miracles point to Jesus as signs, to help people believe in him as **God's Son**.

Any examples?

Here are a few: Jesus fed 5,000 people, and later said, **"I am the bread of life."** Before he healed a blind man he said, **"I am the light of the world."** And before he raised dead Lazarus, he said, **"I am the resurrection and the life."** Each of these signs reveal something of who Jesus was.

Where to find them...

HEALING

Blind Bartimaeus
Mark 10:46–52
Centurion's servant
Luke 7:1–10
Deaf and dumb man
Mark 7:31–37

CASTING OUT DEMONS

Man from Gadara
Mark 5:1–15

RAISING THE DEAD

Lazarus
John 11:1–44
Jairus's daughter
Mark 5:22–24, 35–43

POWER OVER NATURE

Walking on water
John 6: 19–21
Feeding 5,000
Mark 6:35–44

THE RESURRECTION

The greatest miracle
Matthew 28, Mark 16,
Luke 24, John 20.

Jesus: all a myth?

How do we know about Jesus? How can we trust what we read about him? Do we know if he even existed?

Our main sources of information for the life of Jesus come from the writings of **the New Testament itself**. They give us the best chance of understanding Jesus, because some of them were probably written by people who were **eyewitnesses** of Jesus and the early church.

However, the New Testament was written **2,000 years** ago. So how can we know that it's come down to us **accurately**? The evidence for this is actually pretty good...

The earliest complete copy of the New Testament which still exists was made about 300 years after the "autographs" (that is, the original writings of the New Testament).

Oldest New Testament

Autograph writers

In comparison, the earliest complete copy of Julius Caesar's celebrated book, "The Gallic War", was made 900 years after the autographs. This is important, as the longer the gap, the more likely there are to be copying errors.

Oldest Gallic War

Many books which were famous in Roman times have simply vanished, leaving no manuscripts. But there are thousands of manuscripts of the New Testament writings. All of which means we have the best chance of knowing what the original writers actually wrote.

THE BIBLE FROM SCRATCH

And how about outside the New Testament?

The **life** and **crucifixion** of Jesus are reported in several writings outside the New Testament...

Josephus

Josephus was a rebel leader in Galilee during the Jewish revolt against Rome just after the time of Jesus. He later switched sides and ended up living in Rome. He wrote these words around the year AD 90...

About this time lived Jesus, a wise man, a teacher of those who delight in accepting the truth. He attracted many Jews, and also many from the Greek world. He was the so-called Christ. On the accusation of our leading men Pilate condemned him to the cross, but those who were attracted to him from the first did not cease to love him. The race of Christians named after him survives to this day.

Tacitus

Tacitus, a Roman historian, wrote in AD 115–17 about the persecution in AD 64 of Christians in Rome by the Emperor Nero – and he gave this explanation of who Christians were in this bad-tempered passage...

The name Christian comes from Christ, who was executed in the reign of Tiberius by the procurator Pontius Pilate; and the pernicious superstition, suppressed for a while, broke out afresh and spread not only in Judea, the source of the malady, but even throughout Rome itself, where everything vile comes and is feted.

And finally... words written by **Mara bar Serapion** from a prison in Syria in the 2nd or 3rd century...

What advantage did the Jews gain from executing their wise king?

The evidence of the New Testament and other writers has made the idea that Jesus didn't exist a **minority view**.

LUKE

Luke is the only one of the four Gospels to have **a sequel.** The book of Acts continues where Luke leaves off, and together they make up **25 per cent** of the New Testament.

Luke sets the story of Jesus on a **worldwide stage.** His story begins (Luke 1) in the Temple in **Jerusalem** and ends up (Acts 28) in a rented house in **Rome.** Uniquely, Luke shows the connection between the life of Jesus and the growth of **the church**, and it's a story of triumph, as the gospel travels to the heart of the Roman empire.

Luke's Gospel

VOLUME 1

Acts

VOLUME 2

Luke develops a number of important themes in his Gospel and in Acts. One to look out for is the work of the Spirit in the life of Jesus and the church. For example, Jesus begins his ministry by saying...

The Spirit of the Lord is upon me, because he has chosen me to bring good news to the poor. Luke 4:18

You can also see this theme in the day of Pentecost in Acts 2.

Who wrote Luke and Acts?

The **early church** believed the author was Luke, a doctor who travelled with **Paul** on his journeys.

His stated aim (in Luke 1:1–4) was to write an account of Jesus' life that was historically **accurate** and made sense to **non-Jewish** readers.

Luke wrote beautiful Greek, and three of his hymns are still spoken and sung in church – the **Magnificat**, **Benedictus** and **Nunc Dimittis** (Luke 1 and 2).

Another big theme of Luke is the way Jesus **trashed** the social priorities of his time – and, for that matter, of almost every other time. His attitude towards **despised and downtrodden** social groups was revolutionary. Here are three such groups – the **poor**, **social outcasts** and **women**. The stories below are told only by Luke – they don't appear in Matthew, Mark or John.

Shhh! The servants might hear you.

The Poor

In keeping with the Old Testament prophets, Jesus said that God is **on the side of the poor** and has a problem with the rich. The parables of the **rich fool** (Luke 12:16–21) and **Lazarus** (Luke 16:19–31) reveal the deadly danger of wealth. Zacchaeus, a rich and corrupt taxman (in Luke 19) **finds salvation** only when he's given half of all he owns to the poor, and pays back with interest the people he's cheated.

Outcasts

Jesus was **infamous** for mixing with people who were considered **immoral** and **criminal**. He answered his critics by saying these were the people who most needed him. Three of Luke's examples show Jesus' attitude to the outcasts of his time…

■ **Taxmen** (who were hated for their greed) Luke 18:9–14
■ **Samaritans** (a despised ethnic group) Luke 10:30–37
■ **Lepers** (who were feared and driven out of the community) Luke 17:11–19

Do not talk to a woman in the street. No, not even to your own wife!

Religious advice in the time of Jesus

Women

In Jesus' day, women were seen by men as **inferior**. They weren't allowed to testify in court, and no one bothered to educate them. But Jesus treated women **differently**. He taught them alongside the men (Luke 10:38–42). Luke more than anyone else shows us Jesus' **compassion** for women (see Luke 7:36–50).

mary

(mother of Jesus)

She's arguably the **most famous woman in history**, with pictures, icons and statues in millions of homes round the world, and yet Mary gets **amazingly little** airtime in the Bible. Outside the birth stories of Jesus, she's only mentioned a handful of times and speaks just **two lines.** Compared to Paul, Peter and others who also played **key roles**, Mary is practically invisible...

You mean like almost every female character in the Bible?

Just before the year 4 BC, a **peasant girl** living on the eastern edge of the Roman Empire gave birth to a baby boy. She called him **Jesus.** What might have been an obscure, everyday event, actually changed the world.

*Matthew and Luke tell us that **Mary** was a virgin when she conceived Jesus – this supported the key belief that his mother was Mary and his father was God: he was God and man. This is one of the reasons why Mary is so important in the Christian faith.*

*Early tradition tells us that **Joseph** was already old when he married Mary – which is consistent with church teaching that Mary never lost her virginity.*

KEY MOMENTS

- Mary visited by **Gabriel** (Luke 1:26–56)
- The **birth** of Jesus (Matthew 1:18–25)
- Mary presents Jesus in the **Temple** (Luke 2:22–40)
- Jesus in **childhood** (Luke 2:41–52)
- Mary at **Cana** (John 2:1–12)
- Mary at the **crucifixion** (John 19:25–27)
- Mary in the **early church** (Acts 1:14)

Mary was **engaged to Joseph** when she was visited by one of heaven's top angels, the archangel **Gabriel**. Experts say she would have been somewhere between 13 and 18 years old (which was marrying age in those times). The angel brought her **disturbing news...**

Luke 1:31

> You will become pregnant and give birth to a son, and you will name him Jesus.

Mary's faith was **so strong**, she was able to accept God's will for her, despite the disgrace it would bring her as an unmarried, pregnant girl. **Her response** to the angel is still sung today...

Mother of the church

As well as being the mother of Jesus, Mary is believed to be the mother of the church (see John 19:25-27). That's why Catholic Christians have a special devotion to Mary. Her virginal conception of Jesus is celebrated on March 25. Her immaculate conception (that means she was born free from original sin) is celebrated on December 8. And her being taken into heaven, body and soul, is celebrated on the Feast of the Assumption on August 15.

My soul glorifies the Lord and my spirit rejoices in God my Savior, for he has been mindful of the humble state of his servant. From now on all generations will call me blessed, for the Mighty One has done great things for me – holy is his name.

Luke 1:46-49

parables

According to Matthew, Mark and Luke, Jesus wasn't in the habit of boring people with **long sermons**. Instead, he often gave his teaching by telling short, attention-grabbing stories known as **parables**.

The word "parable" has many meanings: picture, riddle, allegory, or story with a **hidden meaning**. Jesus wasn't alone in teaching like this. Some **rabbis** around in his time used parables, and you can also find examples in the **Old Testament**, but Jesus is far and away the best parable-teller you'll find. He was famous for **talking in pictures**.

Let me tell you the one about the exploding wineskin...

Oh yes!

So how did they go down?

The reactions were **a bit mixed.** Many of the parables Jesus told were clearly meant to communicate with ordinary people, and they were **understood** right away. Large crowds heard and enjoyed them. Even his enemies got the point of what he was saying...

The chief priests and the Pharisees heard Jesus' parables and knew he was talking about them...

Matthew 21:45

THE BIBLE FROM SCRATCH

But at other times, the things Jesus said in picture-language **confused** even his closest followers. For example, this from Matthew 15:15–16...

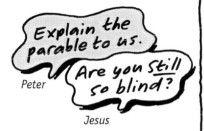

Explain the parable to us.

Peter

Are you *still* so blind?

Jesus

The parables of Jesus are based on **agricultural** life, with a cast including farmworkers, fishermen, house-builders and shepherds, and covering everyday events such as mending clothes, paying workers and losing money. None of Jesus' parables is about life in **the city**.

Animals feature a lot. No fewer than three parables give sheep a starring role: the lost sheep, the sheep and the goats, and the "I am the good shepherd" teaching of Jesus.

 # Find that parable

Read some of the **best-known** parables for yourself, as found in Matthew, Mark and Luke...

	Matthew	Mark	Luke
Rock or sand?	7:24–27		6:47–49
The sower	13:3–8	4:3–8	8:5–8
The weeds in the crop	13:24–30		
Where's the sheep?	18:12–13		15:4–6
Two servants in debt	18:23–34		
A workers' pay dispute	20:1–16		
The evil tenants	21:33–41	12:1–9	20:9–16
The reluctant guests	22:2–14		14:16–24
The 10 girls	25:1–13		
The talents	25:14–30		19:11–27
Sheep or goats?	25:31–46		
The good Samaritan			10:30–37
A friend at midnight			11:5–8
The rich fool			12:16–21
Return of the lost son			15:11–32
A rich man dies			16:19–31
Widow vs judge			18:2–5
A taxman prays			18:10–14

PARTIES &

In Jesus' time, there were many **political** and **religious** parties and groups operating in Palestine, and several of them play a part in the Gospels.

The underlying reality of life was the occupation of Palestine by the Roman **military**, as Judea was a province of the **Roman empire**. While some parties **cooperated** with the Romans in administering the province, others actively **resisted**.

Jesus came into serious **conflict** with the religious groups right from the start. His most famous clashes were with the **Pharisees**, but he also tangled regularly with the **Scribes** and occasionally with the **Sadducees**.

These pages show the five main groupings of the time.

The Scribes – *their job was to preserve and teach the law of Moses, and to act as judges. Their focus on the tiniest details of the law brought them into frequent conflict with Jesus, who accused them of losing the heart of it all.*

The Pharisees – *a minority group with big appeal among the working people, as many of the Pharisees were artisans themselves. Their aim was to help people apply God's Law to every area of life. They opposed revolt against the rule of Rome. See page 198 for more details.*

GROUPS

Sadducees

Zealots

The Zealots – *actively resisted Roman rule, using violence. Today they would be called terrorists. There was no formal Zealot party in Jesus' time, but instead a number of resistance groups. One of Jesus' disciples, Simon the Zealot, had probably been involved.*

Essenes

The Sadducees – *land-owning aristocrats and the political leaders at the time of Jesus. They controlled the Sanhedrin (the Jewish council which tried Jesus) and many of them were priests. They rejected belief in an afterlife, which brought them into dispute with Jesus.*

The Essenes – *a group living as monks near the Dead Sea who withdrew from Jewish society, which they considered corrupt. Although they're not mentioned in the New Testament, some experts think John the Baptist might have grown up as an Essene. They're famous now for producing the Dead Sea Scrolls, discovered in 1948.*

PHARISEES

They were the baddies, weren't they?

According to the Gospels, the Pharisees were the religious group **Jesus clashed with** most strongly. This casts them in the role of "baddies", of course, which is a bit surprising, because there were lots of **good things** about the Pharisees – not least the fact that they were motivated by a deep desire to serve and **please God**.

The Pharisees followed in the footsteps of **Ezra** in the Old Testament. Ezra (see page 94) had stressed the importance of **obeying God's law**, and the Pharisees worked this out in detail, seeking to apply the law to **every area of life**. In effect, what they were aiming at was the renewal of Israel's faith. To do this, they developed a **system of rules** to help people keep the law. They called these rules "a hedge" – the hedge stopped you from accidentally crashing into the law and breaking it.

5,000 THINGS THAT MAKE GOD VERY ANGRY

For example, they laid down 39 "don't do this" rules for keeping the sabbath (the Jewish day of rest). The rules included...

Do not set a broken arm or leg on the sabbath.

Do not carry any burden on the sabbath.

Do not cut your fingernails on the sabbath.

Hmm... sounds a bit over the top. Is that why Jesus disagreed with them so much?

Well, there were several **flashpoints**. Here are just three of them...

The sabbath

Jesus **healed** people and didn't stop his disciples **plucking grain** on the sabbath – both of which went way beyond the "don't cut your fingernails" sort of thinking about the Jewish day of rest. "The sabbath was **made for humankind**, not humankind for the sabbath," said Jesus (Mark 2:27).

Hypocrites!

The hardest and **cruelest words** ever spoken by Jesus were aimed at the Pharisees – you can find the episode in Matthew 23, where he accuses them of **hypocrisy**. The danger of any hyper-spiritual group such as the Pharisees is that they become proud of themselves and scornful of others, and Jesus wasn't alone in **satirizing** their hypocrisy. One Jewish satirist identified several types of Pharisee, including the **shoulder Pharisee**, who displays his good deeds on his shoulder, the **bruised Pharisee**, who walks into a wall rather than look at a woman in the street, and the **pestle Pharisee**, who walks with his head down, like a pestle in a mortar.

Jesus and sinners

The Pharisees were also scandalized that Jesus ate with **tax collectors** and people they called "sinners". While Jesus was interested in **people**, the Pharisees were interested in keeping **the rules**.

Is that why they had him killed?

Actually, they didn't. The Pharisees played no part in the plot to arrest and try Jesus. They're completely absent from the story of his suffering and death, which seems to have been engineered by the authorities in Jerusalem.

As soon as you open John's Gospel, you discover that it's **very different** from Matthew, Mark and Luke...

There aren't as many miracles!

There isn't a single exorcism.

Jesus gives long speeches rather than short, snappy sayings.

Where have all Jesus' great parables gone?

Jesus seems to talk much more about himself!

He's in Jerusalem most of the time, rather than in Galilee.

There's hardly any mention of the kingdom of God.

Whoever wrote John's Gospel must have been using **different sources** of information from those used by the writers of the other three Gospels. But are these sources **better** or **worse**?

It used to be thought that John's sources – and therefore his portrait of Jesus – were worse than those used by Matthew, Mark and Luke. But recent research has shown that John's details are **historically accurate**. So it looks as if John's Gospel is using a stream of stories and teaching which isn't better or worse than the other three Gospels, but just **different**.

John is incredibly valuable as it gives us an independent and alternative view of Jesus.

THE BIBLE FROM SCRATCH

In John's Gospel, Jesus openly declares **who he is**. John includes **seven sayings** of Jesus which begin with the words: **I am...** These "I am" sayings give us different glimpses of Jesus' identity and help us to build up a picture of him. They are...

> **I am the bread of life. He who comes to me will never go hungry, and he who believes in me will never be thirsty.**
> *John 6:35*

> **I am the light of the world. Whoever follows me will never walk in darkness, but will have the light of life.**
> *John 8:12*

> **I am the gate for the sheep.**
> *John 10:7*

> **I am the resurrection and the life. He who believes in me will live, even though he dies; and whoever lives and believes in me will never die.**
> *John 11:25–26*

> **I am the good shepherd. The good shepherd lays down his life for the sheep.**
> *John 10:11*

> **I am the way and the truth and the life.**
> *John 14:6*

> **I am the true vine and my Father is the gardener.**
> *John 15:1*

Hmm. "I am". Where have I heard that before?

In the Old Testament, this is how God speaks about himself. In Exodus 3:14, God says to Moses, "I AM WHO I AM. This is what you are to say to the Israelites: 'I AM has sent me to you.'" Jesus is making a pretty huge claim here.

THE FATHER

our Father in heaven......

Jesus talked about God as a **father** in the other three Gospels, but in John he gives the fullest teaching about his relationship to **God the Father** to be found in the four Gospels.

He says he was **sent by** the Father, that he is the only **way to** the Father, and (most shocking of all to his listeners) he said...

I and the Father are one.

John 10:30

These passages in John were later **crucial** to the church in formulating belief in God as a **trinity** of Father, Son and Holy Spirit.

THE HERODS

The **Herod dynasty** ruled Palestine as part of the Roman empire throughout the time of the New Testament. The family was **mafia-like** in its suspicions, intrigues, betrayals and violence, with frequent **intermarrying** of uncles and even great-uncles with nieces. Two of the Herods feature strongly in the **Gospels**...

The Herod family tree opposite shows only a fraction of the family, which was big, complicated and quarrelsome.

The Great

Herod the Great was ambitious, commanding and **supremely suspicious** – he killed one of his wives and several of his children when he thought they were plotting against him. His suspicions when the **wise men** visited him at the birth of Jesus ring true to what we know about him.

Herod rebuilt the Jerusalem Temple and built luxury palaces for himself – the one at Masada includes his famous swimming pool.

Antipas

Herod Antipas, one of the younger sons of Herod the Great, appears in the Gospels in two places: the **death of John** the Baptist and the **death of Jesus**.

Herod had John arrested when John started preaching against his marriage to **Herodias** (she had been his brother's wife). He had John executed on his birthday, after a **dramatic dance** by his wife's daughter – see Mark 6:14–29.

Herod also comes into the story of **Jesus' trial** (Luke 23:6–12). **Pilate** sent Jesus to him for questioning. Herod was delighted as he wanted to see a miracle or two, but Jesus refused even to speak. Herod sent him back to Pilate **dressed as a king**.

That fox

Jesus' description of Herod in Luke 13:32

Herod the Great

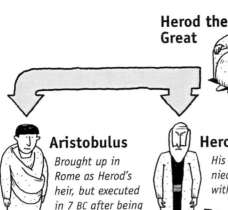

King of the Jews (40–4 BC), built the Temple, tried to kill Jesus as a baby

Aristobulus

Brought up in Rome as Herod's heir, but executed in 7 BC after being framed for treason

Herod-Philip

His wife (who was also his niece) Herodias ran off with Herod Antipas

Herod Antipas

Ruler of Galilee and Peraea until AD 39, Herod Antipas had John the Baptist executed for condemning his marriage to Herodias, and he questioned Jesus on the night before his crucifixion

Herod I Agrippa

Ruler of the kingdom of Herod the Great AD 41–44, his sudden death is recorded in Acts 12:20–23

Herodias

Mother of Salome (Herod-Philip was the father), Herodias nursed a grudge against John the Baptist

Agrippa II

The ruler of territories NE of Palestine until AD 100, Agrippa interviewed Paul and joked, "You're almost persuading me to become a Christian" (Acts 26:28)

Salome

Danced so sexily for Herod Antipas on his birthday that he promised her up to half his kingdom... but her mother told her to ask for the head of John the Baptist instead

The Devil

Satan (aka the devil) doesn't trouble the Old Testament very much, confining himself mainly to an enigmatic appearance in chapters 1 and 2 of the book of Job. In those chapters, Satan is a member of God's royal court, acting as his special **prosecutor**. His appearance sets the agenda for the book, though, as he tries to engineer the **downfall of Job**, a good man admired by God himself.

Things take off right after the **baptism** of Jesus, when he's **tempted** by the devil in the desert (see Luke 4:1-13). Here, the Devil appears as a **truly malevolent** power, determined to wreck Jesus' mission.

So when do things...er... hot up?

Jesus (plus Paul and Peter, in their letters) talks about the devil not only as someone who tempts individuals, but as the **cosmic enemy** of God and the **origin of evil** in the world. Jesus' death broke his power, and he will finally be **destroyed** at the end of time.

Your enemy the devil prowls around like a roaring lion looking for someone to devour.

1 Peter 5:8

GIVING THE DEVIL A BAD NAME

The most common names for the devil are...

Beelzebub – an insulting name used by Jesus, which means "Lord of the flies" (Matthew 12:27–28).

Devil – comes from a Greek word, "diabolos", which is where we get the word "diabolical" (see James 4:7).

Evil One – often used in the New Testament as an alternative to "devil" (e.g. Ephesians 6:16).

Satan – literally means "the accuser". This name highlights Satan's role as a cunning adversary (Revelation 12:9).

DEATH AND RESURRECTION

The most famous execution in history is recorded near the end of all four Gospels.

Jesus was **betrayed** by Judas, one of his close followers. He was **tried** by the religious establishment, **sentenced** by Pontius Pilate, the local governor, and **crucified** by Roman soldiers.

Read the accounts of the crucifixion in Matthew 27, Mark 15, Luke 23 and John 19

Jesus was put to death on a **Friday.** Early on the **Sunday morning**, his tomb was discovered empty. All four Gospels record different stories about the resurrection of Jesus...

MATTHEW

■ *Jesus appears to **Mary Magdalene** outside the tomb (Matthew 28:1–10)*

■ *Jesus appears to the remaining **11 disciples** in Galilee (Matthew 28:16–20)*

LUKE

■ *Mary Magdalene and other women find the empty tomb and see two angels who say Jesus is alive (Luke 24:1–12)*

■ ***Two disciples** encounter the risen Jesus while walking to the village of **Emmaus** (Luke 24:13–35)*

■ *Jesus appears to the **11 disciples** in Jerusalem (Luke 24:36–49)*

MARK

■ ***Mary Magdalene** and other women find the tomb of Jesus empty and an angel tells them Jesus is risen (Mark 16:1–8)*

JOHN

■ ***Mary Magdalene** finds the tomb empty and runs to tell **Peter** and another disciple, who race to the tomb, but find nothing (John 20:1–10)*

■ *Jesus appears to **Mary Magdalene** (John 20:11–18).*

■ *Jesus appears to doubting **Thomas** (John 20:24–29).*

■ *Jesus appears to **seven disciples** at the Sea of Galilee (John 21:1–24).*

Judas

THE BETRAYAL

What Judas did in the final days of Jesus' life...

- *Angry at Jesus being anointed in Bethany (John 12:1–8)*

- *Agrees a price with the chief priests to betray Jesus (Matthew 26:14–16)*

- *Leaves the Last Supper early (John 13:18–30)*

- *Betrays Jesus with a kiss (Matthew 26:47–50)*

- *Tries to return the money and then commits suicide (Matthew 27:3–10)*

Judas, who left to go to the place where he belongs.

The final verdict of the first Christians on Judas (Acts 1:25)

It's one of the **supreme twists** in the story of Jesus that he was betrayed into the hands of his enemies by a **friend**, and that the friend used the symbol of love – a **kiss** – to do it. Judas Iscariot was one of the 12 disciples and had been with Jesus from the beginning. So **what made him do it?** Here are some of the different theories...

Money

The Gospels suggest he did it partly for **the money**. Judas looked after the disciples' money-bag and was said to steal from it (John 12:6). He was paid **30 silver coins** for informing on Jesus.

Fear

Another theory: Judas was **afraid** of what the authorities might do to the disciples if Jesus was arrested. That's why he sold Jesus to them.

Politics

Some say Judas had always seen Jesus as a **political messiah** (see page 185). When Jesus refused to take the role, Judas created **a crisis** to force Jesus to declare himself. He committed suicide when it all went badly wrong.

Evil

One of the oldest explanations was that Judas was prompted by **the devil**: "Satan entered Judas" (Luke 22:3, John 13:27).

Pilate

Pontius Pilate was **Governor of Judea** (a Roman province) in AD 26–36. Judea was violent and difficult to govern, and Pilate was violent and difficult himself, which made his time in charge of the province **extremely troubled.** He gained a reputation for insensitivity, corruption and antagonizing the population. The 1st-century Jewish historian, **Philo**, complained about...

Pilate's most famous "untried prisoner" was Jesus, who was brought before him on a trumped-up charge of **inciting rebellion** against the Roman emperor. The four Gospels paint Pilate as a **weak character** who was **pressured** into sentencing Jesus to death.

His opponents exploited a known weakness of his: he was afraid of **bad reports** reaching the emperor. This explains why he caved after the crowd shouted...

66 ... his venality, his violence, his thefts, his assaults, his abusive behaviour, his frequent executions of untried prisoners, and his endless savage ferocity... **99**

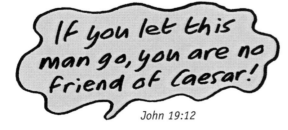

If you let this man go, you are no friend of Caesar!

John 19:12

Pilate took revenge on the leaders who had called for Jesus' execution by nailing a notice on Jesus' cross, proclaiming him "King of the Jews". A few years later, Pilate was recalled to Rome after he committed a massacre, and he was banished to France.

KING OF THE JEWS

GOSPEL HIGHLIGHTS

Looking for some of the most **dramatic moments** from the Gospels? If so, look no further...

☐ Caught in a storm (Mark 4:37–41)

☐ The demon-possessed man of the tombs (Mark 5:1–15)

☐ Jesus walks on water, while Peter sinks (Matthew 14:22–33)

☐ Jesus is challenged to condemn a woman to death (John 8:2–11)

☐ Peter denies knowing Jesus (Luke 22:54–62)

☐ Jesus is crucified (Luke 23:32–49)

☐ Mary mistakes Jesus for a gardener (John 20:11–18)

Waterwings, anyone?

THE CHURCH

While **Matthew, Mark** and **John** put down their pens after finishing their Gospels, **Luke** carried on writing and produced a book called The Acts of the Apostles. Because of him, we can follow the story from Jesus to the **early church** and from Nazareth to **Rome**.

The book of Acts tells how the good news of Jesus packed its bags, left its homeland and travelled into the world.

ACTS

How do you get from **this**...

... to **this**?

How we got from the life and teaching of Jesus to **the church** as it is today is a long (and sometimes depressing) story. The book of Acts provides a vital **first link**, though, connecting up Jesus with the **first Christians** and the **first churches**.

Acts was written as the **sequel** to Luke's Gospel and together they show the transition from **Jesus** to the **church**...

In Luke, Jesus reaches out to the different people around him, including the poor and marginalized, proclaiming the arrival of God's kingdom.

In Acts, it's the followers of Jesus who reach out to the world around them – not just the Jewish world, but the wide world of the Roman empire.

Jesus himself provides the link between **his mission** and the **church's mission**. At the end of Luke (Luke 24:48) he tells the disciples...

You are Witnesses...

... and at the beginning of Acts (Acts 1:8) he pushes this thought further by saying...

You will be my witnesses in Jerusalem, and in all Judea and Samaria, and to the ends of the earth.

But the church doesn't come into being simply by **Jesus talking** about it – it happens when the **Holy Spirit** falls on the first believers. Just as Jesus lived his life in the power of the Spirit (in Luke), so the church also **lives in the Spirit**, continuing Jesus' mission in the world (in Acts). If you read **Luke and Acts** together, you can see the connections.

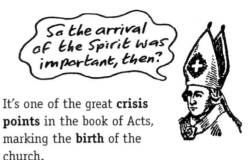

So the arrival of the Spirit was important, then?

It's one of the great **crisis points** in the book of Acts, marking the **birth** of the church.

The descent of the Spirit **changes everything**. It's as though the first believers have received the jolt of **energy** they needed to carry out what Jesus told them to do.

They start spreading the good news in **Jerusalem**...

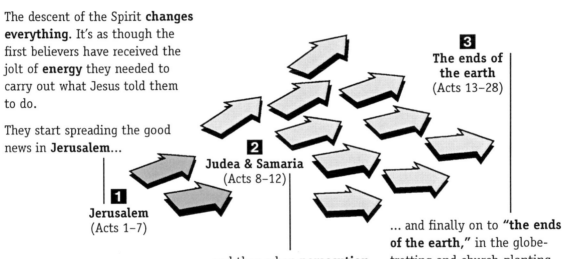

3
The ends of the earth
(Acts 13–28)

2
Judea & Samaria
(Acts 8–12)

1
Jerusalem
(Acts 1–7)

... and then when **persecution** breaks out against them in Jerusalem, they scatter, taking the good news to **Judea** and **Samaria**...

... and finally on to **"the ends of the earth,"** in the globe-trotting and church-planting of **Paul** in what are now Turkey and Greece. By the end of the story of Acts, what had started as a small Jewish sect in Galilee has gone international, including **Jews** and **non-Jews** across the Roman world.

THE ROMANS

Roman rule was the underlying **fact of life** for people living in the Mediterranean world of the 1st century AD. Measured from north to south, it stretched from Hadrian's Wall on the borders of **Scotland** to the sands of the **Sahara** Desert. And from west to east, it ran from the Atlantic coast of **Spain** to the shores of the **Red Sea**.

At its height, the empire included over **100 million** people and was patrolled by a professional army numbering almost half a million soldiers. In each province of the empire, the Roman authorities worked alongside local rulers to maintain **public order**, administer **justice** and raise **taxes**. Because the empire brought order and stability to such a large region, it was great for business.

Occupying Judea

In the time of the New Testament, **Judea** was a province of the Roman empire. This meant that it was a country under **military occupation**, with Roman troops and fortresses across the land. This suited some sections of Jewish society, such as the **Sadducees**, who cooperated with the Romans and grew **wealthy**. But for others, such as the **Zealots**, the Romans were hated and opposed.

So what did the first Christians think about the Roman empire?

Well, they saw it in **two ways** (see next page)...

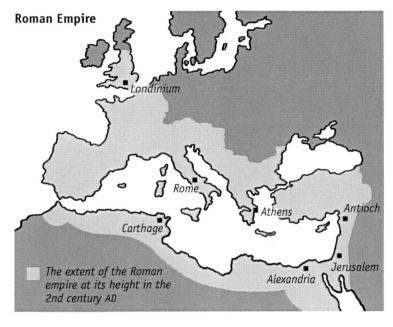

Roman Empire

Londinium

Rome

Carthage

Athens

Antioch

Alexandria

Jerusalem

The extent of the Roman empire at its height in the 2nd century AD

Good

In many ways the Roman empire helped to speed the Christian good news around the world, because of...

- **Roman roads** – made travel fast.
- **Greek** – the language used throughout the empire.
- **Pax Romana** – the "Roman peace" meant life was stable and secure.

So there was a **friendly attitude** among Christians towards the empire.

Paul even used Roman images, such as a soldier's battle-dress in his teaching: "put on the whole armour of God" (Ephesians 6:11).

Evil

On the other hand, Christians were frequently **in trouble** with the empire. Their enemies accused them of **treason** against the emperor...

> They are defying Caesar's decrees, saying there is another king, one called Jesus.

Acts 17:7

Christians answered this by saying that they could **worship** Jesus and **obey** the emperor.

But the crunch came when they were told to worship **the emperor** instead of Jesus. This happened in the reign of **Domitian** (from AD 81). Persecution and death followed for countless Christians.

The book of **Revelation**, written in that time of persecution, characterizes Rome as **evil**. It says that Rome, like Babylon in the Old Testament, would be **judged** and **destroyed** by God.

PETER

He was some sort of fisherman, wasn't he?

Simon Peter is one of the most colorful characters of the New Testament. He was a **fisherman** with his brother **Andrew** on the Sea of Galilee. He was married, had a strong North country accent (Matthew 26:73), and was warm, quick and impulsive by nature. Jesus called him to be one of the **twelve disciples** and he quickly became one of Jesus' most trusted friends. Jesus gave him a nickname: **the rock** (the Greek word "petros").

Peter's faith, like his temperament, could **rise** to the heights and **sink** to the depths (sometimes in the same afternoon). These quotes from Jesus say it all...

The earliest images of Peter show him with white curly hair and a beard.

Blessed are you, Simon, son of John!

When Peter confessed Jesus to be the Son of God (Matthew 16:17)

Out of my sight, Satan! You are a stumbling block to me!

Jesus' words to Peter, after Peter tried to dissuade him from going to Jerusalem to die (Matthew 16:23)

Peter's relationship with Jesus could be a bit stormy and it was often in the spotlight. We know more about their relationship than that of any of the **other disciples** of Jesus.

Peter has some of the **big moments** of the New Testament...

Halfway through his ministry, Jesus asked the disciples, "Who do you think I am?" Peter replied, "The Messiah, the son of the living God" (see Matthew 16:13–20). For this leap of faith, Jesus appointed Peter leader of the church.

After Jesus' arrest, Peter, scared for his life, denied three times that he knew Jesus (Mark 14:66–72). His loyalty was later tested by Jesus three times (John 21:15–19), and he was forgiven.

On the Day of Pentecost, when the Spirit fell on the first believers, Peter preached to the crowd and large numbers of them became Christians (Acts 2:14–41).

One of the biggest issues facing the early church was whether it was for Jews only, or also for Gentiles (non-Jews). In the middle of the fierce debate this provoked, Peter had a strange vision which changed his Jews-only beliefs (Acts 10:9–16).

The church teaches that the Holy Father, **the Pope**, is the direct **successor of Peter** – the one Christ called the Rock, the foundation of the church. The Pope is called the "Vicar" (or representative) of Christ and the Pastor of the Universal Church, entrusted with the **keys of the kingdom of heaven** (Matthew 16:17-19) and commanded by Christ to "feed my sheep" (John 21:15-17).

Peter & Paul

There was **friction** in the relationship of Peter and Paul and it shows in the New Testament. Paul accused Peter of being **inconsistent** about the Jewish-Gentile issue, and says he confronted Peter face to face on the issue (Galatians 2:9–14).

According to tradition, Peter and Paul were both killed in the savage **persecution** of Christians by the Emperor **Nero**, around AD 64. While Paul was beheaded, Peter was **crucified** upside down.

Emperor Nero

PAUL

Paul (aka 'the Apostle Paul') is the **most energetic** person in the New Testament. Over his 30-year career, he **travelled** the Roman empire, **preached** the good news, **founded** churches, **suffered** persecution and imprisonment, **debated** with philosophers... and in his spare time, wrote many of **the letters** that make up the bulk of the New Testament.

According to a 2nd-century book called **The Acts of Paul**, Paul was... "a man small of stature, with a bald head and crooked legs, in a good state of body, with eyebrows meeting and nose somewhat hooked, full of grace; for now he appeared like a man, and now he had the face of an angel."

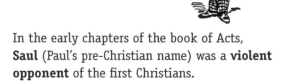

But Paul wasn't one of the original 12 disciples – so how did he get in on the act?

Paul is shown looking like this from the earliest times.

In the early chapters of the book of Acts, **Saul** (Paul's pre-Christian name) was a **violent opponent** of the first Christians.

He was a **Pharisee**, and was given authority by the religious establishment in Jerusalem to root out and arrest Christians, and he voted to have some killed (he tells his story in Acts 26:9–11). His persecution of Christians was **obsessive**.

But all that changed in Acts 9, when Paul had the original **road to Damascus** experience.

While Paul was travelling to **Damascus** on yet another seek-and-destroy mission against Christians, he had, in his own words, **a heavenly vision** of the risen Jesus. In the vision, which threw him to the ground and temporarily blinded him, **Jesus** asked him a simple question...

Saul, Saul, why do you persecute me?

Acts 9:4

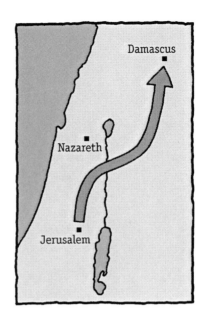

The experience changed Paul for ever. He was **baptized** and immediately started **preaching** in the synagogues of Damascus that Jesus was the Son of God. This event had an impact on Paul in **three ways**...

He was convinced **he had met Jesus**, alive from the dead. Just as Jesus had appeared to Peter, John and the rest, so now he had appeared to Paul.

Just as Paul's experience was the same as the apostles, he claimed the same status as them: **he too was an apostle**, even if he was a late arrival at the party (read what he said for yourself in 1 Corinthians 15:3–11).

Paul said that his call was as the **apostle to the gentiles** (non-Jews), a call which he remarkably fulfilled in his journeys through what are now Turkey and Greece.

Paul has always been **controversial.** The news of his conversion was initially greeted with **shock and suspicion**, and he gained instant **celebrity** among the first Christians...

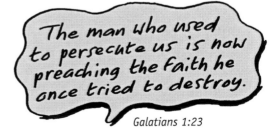

The man who used to persecute us is now preaching the faith he once tried to destroy.

Galatians 1:23

LETTERS

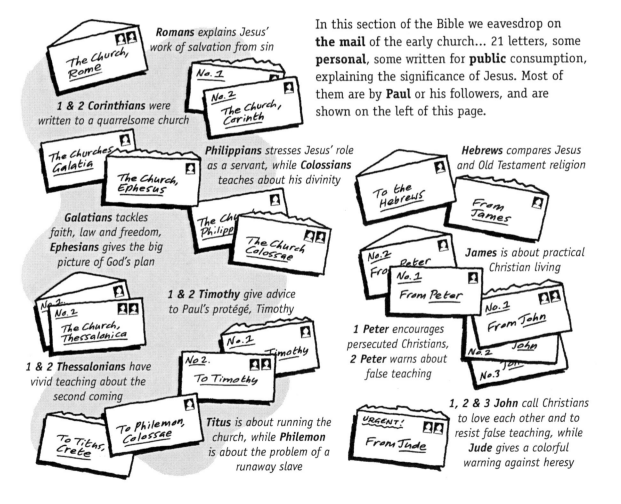

Romans explains Jesus' work of salvation from sin

The Church, Rome

1 & 2 Corinthians were written to a quarrelsome church

No. 1

No. 2 The Church, Corinth

In this section of the Bible we eavesdrop on **the mail** of the early church... 21 letters, some **personal**, some written for **public** consumption, explaining the significance of Jesus. Most of them are by **Paul** or his followers, and are shown on the left of this page.

The Churches Galatia

The Church, Ephesus

Philippians stresses Jesus' role as a servant, while **Colossians** teaches about his divinity

The Church Philipp

The Church Colossae

Galatians tackles faith, law and freedom, **Ephesians** gives the big picture of God's plan

Hebrews compares Jesus and Old Testament religion

To the Hebrews

From James

James is about practical Christian living

No. 2 The Church, Thessalonica

1 & 2 Timothy give advice to Paul's protégé, Timothy

No. 1 Timothy

No 2. To Timothy

No. 2 From Peter

No. 1 From Peter

No. 1 From John

No. 2 John

No. 3 John

1 & 2 Thessalonians have vivid teaching about the second coming

1 Peter encourages persecuted Christians, **2 Peter** warns about false teaching

To Titus, Crete

To Philemon, Colossae

Titus is about running the church, while **Philemon** is about the problem of a runaway slave

URGENT! From Jude

1, 2 & 3 John call Christians to love each other and to resist false teaching, while **Jude** gives a colorful warning against heresy

INTRO

Over **one-third** of the New Testament contains the mail of the early church. There are 21 letters, written to groups and individuals in **the early years** following the death of Jesus. Some of them are long and complicated, while others are short and straightforward – one of them could be written on a **postcard** (admittedly in tiny writing)...

So why did they write them?

Most of them were written to fix the **big problems** facing the young churches. The letters are full of details about real people and situations – and yet they also speak to us today.

They were written by people who were on the move, which is why they're often so **down-to-earth** and **practical**. And they were written for many reasons – for example, to...

- combat **wrong ideas** (Galatians, Colossians)
- tackle **crises** in the churches (1 & 2 Corinthians)
- explain important **teaching** (Romans, Hebrews)
- encourage Christians **under pressure** (1 Peter)
- make a **personal appeal** (Philemon, 3 John)

The letters were the first parts of the New Testament to be written. 1 Thessalonians, written by Paul to a church in northern Greece, is reckoned to be earliest.

It was written around AD 50, some 20 years after the crucifixion of Jesus. It beat the writing of the earliest of the four Gospels (Mark) by about 20 years.

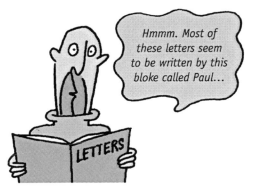

Hmmm. Most of these letters seem to be written by this bloke called Paul...

After Jesus himself, Paul is the **big figure** of the New Testament. He wasn't one of the 12 disciples – in fact, he actively tried to **destroy** the Christian faith, which was hardly a brilliant start. But he was **dramatically converted** (see page 217) and became famous as the **apostle to the Gentiles**, travelling the Mediterranean world of his time.

Paul was an **ambitious pioneer.** His journeys (into what are now Turkey, Greece, Italy and Spain) put churches in places the other followers of Jesus wouldn't have dreamed about. His letters (and those **written in his name** by other writers – see page 225) were a lifeline to those first churches as they struggled to grow up in a hostile world. They fall into **four categories**...

For a list of the non-Paul letters, see the right-hand side of page 219...

← **THIS WAY**

FIRST POST

1 + 2 THESSALONIANS

MAIN DELIVERY

ROMANS 1 + 2 CORINTHIANS GALATIANS

PRISON POST

EPHESIANS PHILIPPIANS COLOSSIANS PHILEMON

FINAL POST

1 + 2 TIMOTHY TITUS

Letters written to one of the first churches founded by Paul

Paul's heavy-hitters... his mature stuff with lots of big themes

These letters were written from prison, probably in Rome

These last letters reflect Paul's experience at the end of his life

ROMANS

Romans is one of the **major books** of the Bible. It's the longest of Paul's letters, and in it he goes right to the heart of the Christian faith, explaining **why Jesus died**, and what his death and resurrection mean.

Why did Paul write it?

The letter was written around **AD 55**, when Paul was staying in **Corinth**. For a long time he had wanted to visit the Christians of Rome, and when he wrote his letter, he was hopeful that he would now at last be able to make the journey to see them.

So...?

So Paul wrote to **introduce** himself and his message to them. What he produced was a comprehensive and detailed **statement of the gospel** as he preached it, something he didn't do in any other letter. For that reason, Romans is like a **manual** of salvation and the Christian life. It makes essential reading.

THE BIBLE FROM SCRATCH

Romans isn't a light read. Paul tackles some big themes, and he develops his **complex arguments** over several chapters, making frequent connections with the **Old Testament.** Here's roughly how his thinking goes in the important first half of the letter...

Over three blistering chapters (Romans 1:18 through to 3:20), Paul lays into the **failures and evils** of the human race, which he says is "filled with every kind of wickedness, evil, greed and depravity." Everyone has **sinned,** Paul concludes, and everyone is in the fearful situation of being under the **righteous judgment** of God.

Against this dark backdrop, Paul now starts to proclaim his gospel (in Romans 3:21 to the end of Romans 5). The **death of Christ** has changed everything, he says. Although we deserve to receive God's judgment for our sins, Jesus **receives it instead** by dying on the cross. When we put our faith in him, we are **justified** and **made righteous** before God. "Just at the right time, when we were still powerless, Christ died for the ungodly," says Paul.

Being put right with God liberates us for a **new way of life** (Romans 6–8). "Count yourselves dead to sin but alive to God in Christ Jesus," says Paul. Even though we still have to struggle to resist sin, the **Spirit** lives within us, giving us the power to overcome sin and live as sons and daughters of God.

In the second half of Romans, Paul covers the problem of Israel (Romans 9–11) and talks about practical issues.

THE BIBLE FROM SCRATCH

PAUL

THE TRAVELLER

Paul couldn't have picked **a better time**, in the ancient world, to have done his extensive travelling. There were a lot of factors that made travel in the Roman world relatively easy. There was **peace** throughout the empire. **Frontiers** were not difficult to cross. The seas were **pirate-free**. And **Roman roads** were straight, quick and went just about everywhere.

So what was it like to travel in those days?

On the road, Paul and his companions would have been passed by chariots carrying the imperial post, slowly moving passenger coaches, and elegant carriages for the wealthy. Paul himself probably travelled **on foot** or **by mule**, covering about 20 miles (32 km) each day.

Travel could be very uncomfortable. In a rare passage, Paul moans about the conditions...

> **In my many travels I have been in danger from floods and robbers... I have often been without enough food, shelter or clothing.**
>
> *2 Corinthians 11:26-27*

So where did they sleep at night?

Paul was a **tent-maker** by trade (Acts 18:3), so he may have joined the many people who camped by the side of the road at night.

Paul also travelled **by sea**, usually during the safe sailing season (June to September). **His shipwreck** in Acts 27, during an October voyage, is one of the most exciting accounts we have of an ancient shipwreck.

WHO WROTE WHAT?

Who wrote all these letters?

Oh dear! I wish you hadn't asked that!

Several New Testament letters were **probably not** written by the people named as their authors. Many experts believe that several of the letters apparently by **Paul**, for example, were written by **other people**, mainly because the style of writing and the language is very different from the letters which were obviously by Paul.

There are other books of the Bible like this, too – such as **Isaiah** (page 122), which was written by more than one author, and the **Wisdom of Solomon** (page 116), which was written several hundred years after King Solomon.

But often the very first verse of the letters say they're from Paul or Peter. Are you saying that's a lie?

No. It sounds strange now, but it was quite common in ancient times for an unknown writer to write **under the name** of a famous author he admired, or whose teaching he followed. For example, a writer may have wanted to put the message God had given him in Paul's name, because he felt **unworthy** to speak for himself.

Or he may have included so many quotes from the famous author, that he credited the whole of his writing to the author, to avoid being accused of plagiarism. To us, all this looks rather like **forgery**, but at the time, it was an **acceptable** way of doing things.

To find out which letters may have been written under an alias, see the individual letter introductions.

The Church Ephesus

Crete

1 CORINTHIANS

1 Corinthians is a letter written by Paul to the **most stormy** church of New Testament times. The church was being torn apart by vicious **arguments**, **immorality** and **quarrelling groups.** The situation was almost out of control, and Paul's letters to them (there were **four** letters in all) are an attempt at fire-fighting.

GREECE

Athens

Corinth

The story so far...

In late AD 50 or 51, Paul **arrived in Corinth** – he was probably the first Christian ever to set foot in the city. He stayed **18 months** and established a church there. Acts 18:1–17 describes this visit in detail.

But why did he stay so long?

Because Corinth was one of the **great cities** of the Roman empire. All the main east-west trade routes passed through Corinth, so it was always **full of people** on the move. It was also a natural stopping-off point for tired businessmen seeking a little relaxation. Corinth was therefore infamous for its **low moral standards**.

Paul took time to establish a church there so that it would be well-protected against the **pressures and temptations** of the city. But he also did it because he knew that a great trading place like Corinth could also become strategic for **exporting** the Christian message.

Unfortunately, despite Paul's careful preparation, the young church **quickly** developed **serious problems.** So Paul sent them a letter (this was before 1 Corinthians). This letter no longer exists, but since it was written before 1 Corinthians, we'll call it **0 Corinthians.** Paul mentions this **missing letter** in 1 Corinthians...

I wrote to you in my letter not to associate with sexually immoral persons...

1 Corinthians 5:9

After Paul wrote and sent 0 Corinthians, **two things** happened...

1 A small number of people from Corinth turned up in **Ephesus,** where Paul was staying (see 1 Corinthians 1:11). They brought **bad news** about the church...

- **Warring groups** were developing
- A man had married his widowed **stepmother**
- Christians were taking each other **to court**
- Their meetings had become **drunken feasts** for the rich, while poorer Christians went hungry

BY SHIP

The "Apostle" Paul
Near Hall of Tyrranus
EPHESUS

2 Almost at the same time, a **letter** arrived from the Corinthians (see 1 Corinthians 7:1). Their letter (which also no longer exists) was **full of questions** asking Paul's advice...

1. How should Christians think about **marriage, sex and divorce**?
2. Should we **eat meat** that's been used in pagan worship?
3. How should **women dress**? And can they be **leaders** in the church?
4. What about **gifts** from the Holy Spirit?
5. What does the **resurrection** mean? Surely the dead won't be raised to life?

NEXT PAGE

Any chance of you telling us what's actually in 1 Corinthians?

OK... this is what Paul did. He wrote them a **second letter.** This is the one we know as 1 Corinthians.

Paul started his letter (in **chapters 1–6**) with the report he had heard from the small group of people who came to see him in Ephesus. He wrote extremely strongly, using **ridicule** and **sarcasm** to point out the terrible danger they were in.

for example →

Already you have all you want! Already you have become rich! You have become kings – and that without us!

1 Corinthians 4:8

Then from the beginning of **chapter 7**, Paul started to answer the questions in the letter the Corinthians had sent him, dealing with **marriage, food offered to idols, spiritual gifts, the Lord's Supper** and other issues.

1 Corinthians, written in the heat of a difficult situation, is priceless for the teaching it gives. It's probably **best known** for three great passages:

- Chapter 11 (instructions on the **eucharist**)
- Chapter 13 (on the prime importance of **love**)
- Chapter 15 (on the **resurrection**)

And what was the result of all this?

The Corinthians weren't at all grateful for Paul's letter. They took it badly. Read on for the continuing saga...

2 CORINTHIANS

Paul's second letter to the Christians in Corinth, Greece, is the **final episode** in a long story. To take it from the beginning, turn back to page 226 and start from **1 Corinthians**.

So what happened next?

Paul's letter **bombed** in Corinth. In response, Paul took a ship to make a short, **emergency visit** – sailing 300 miles across the Aegean Sea. Paul hoped to sort out the problems by speaking to the Corinthians **face to face**, but the visit was unpleasant and proved to be a failure. The problems of quarrelling and division in the church were **as bad as ever**.

MEGA-URGENT
The Christians
22 Aphrodite Place
CORINTH

So Paul wrote **another** letter (no copies of it have survived). It was written in between 1 and 2 Corinthians, so we can call it **One-and-a-half Corinthians**. It's often called Paul's "severe letter" (see 2 Corinthians 2:4). Paul hoped his harsh words would shock the Corinthians to their senses. One of his trusted workers, **Titus**, took this fateful letter to Corinth.

And finally...

Paul was **anxious** to hear how the Corinthians would react to his letter... and finally, after writing three letters, he had **good news**. They had taken his severe letter to heart and changed their ways (see 2 Corinthians 7:5–16).

The letter we know as 2 Corinthians is Paul's **joyful response**. It's one of his most **personal** letters and reveals a lot about his feelings as he went through doubt, disappointment and (ultimately) triumph with the Corinthian Christians.

PAUL

ARRIVES IN EUROPE

Paul's second (and greatest) journey to plant churches lasted **three years** – from around AD 49–52. Paul travelled with **Silas**, and they picked up **Timothy** and **Luke** along the way.

The plan was to **revisit the churches** Paul had planted a year earlier in the Roman province of **Galatia** (modern-day northern Turkey), but they ended up in the town of Troas, the most western town in Asia Minor.

There, Paul had **a vision** in the night of a Greek man begging him...

> Come over to Macedonia and help us!
>
> Acts 16:9

... which is how the Christian faith arrived in **Europe** for the first time.

Follow the numbers on the map to trace the journey of Paul and his companions through Turkey and Greece.

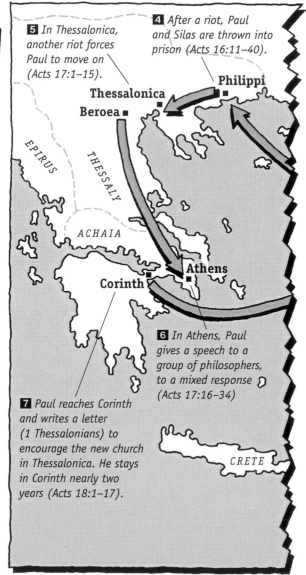

5 *In Thessalonica, another riot forces Paul to move on (Acts 17:1–15).*

4 *After a riot, Paul and Silas are thrown into prison (Acts 16:11–40).*

6 *In Athens, Paul gives a speech to a group of philosophers, to a mixed response (Acts 17:16–34)*

7 *Paul reaches Corinth and writes a letter (1 Thessalonians) to encourage the new church in Thessalonica. He stays in Corinth nearly two years (Acts 18:1–17).*

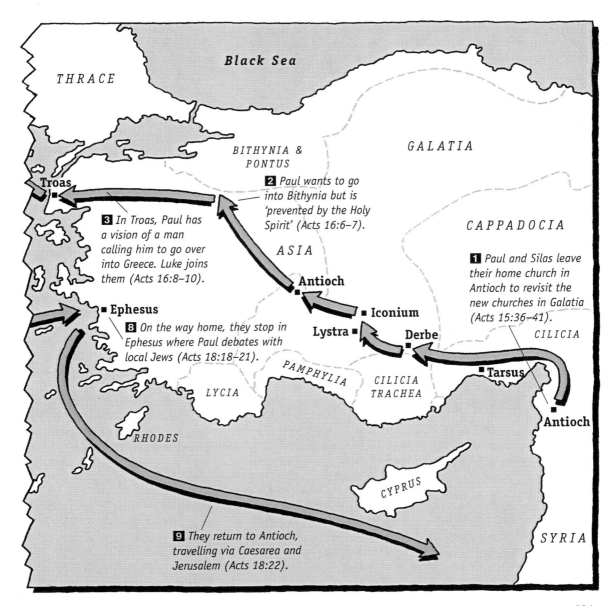

THRACE

Black Sea

BITHYNIA & PONTUS

GALATIA

CAPPADOCIA

Troas

2 *Paul wants to go into Bithynia but is 'prevented by the Holy Spirit' (Acts 16:6–7).*

3 *In Troas, Paul has a vision of a man calling him to go over into Greece. Luke joins them (Acts 16:8–10).*

ASIA

1 *Paul and Silas leave their home church in Antioch to revisit the new churches in Galatia (Acts 15:36–41).*

Antioch

Ephesus

Iconium

Lystra

Derbe

CILICIA

8 *On the way home, they stop in Ephesus where Paul debates with local Jews (Acts 18:18–21).*

PAMPHYLIA

CILICIA TRACHEA

Tarsus

LYCIA

Antioch

RHODES

CYPRUS

9 *They return to Antioch, travelling via Caesarea and Jerusalem (Acts 18:22).*

SYRIA

Galatians

Like **1 and 2 Corinthians**, Paul's letter to the Galatians was written in response to a **quarrel**. It all started about 13 years after the time of Jesus...

Paul set out on his **first preaching journey**, taking his friend Barnabas with him. They headed into **Galatia**, preaching in four towns, and groups of Christians were formed there (Acts 13–14). These new Galatian Christians came from both **Jewish** and **non-Jewish** backgrounds.

Galatia was a Roman province in what is now east Turkey.

So why did that cause a quarrel?

Because the question of what to do with **non-Jews** who were becoming Christians was the **hottest issue** in the early church. The first Christians were very divided about it. Here are the **two opposed** points of view...

God treats Jews and non-Jews in the same way. He wants everyone to receive new life by faith in Jesus.

This is the message that Paul preached

If non-Jews want to become Christians, they must obey the Law of Moses and be circumcised. They must become Jews first!

This is what a group known as "the Judaizers" demanded – see Acts 15:5

This argument went right to the heart of what the new faith was all about – was it for **Jews only**, or for people of **every race**? Were you saved by simply **believing in Jesus**, or by obeying the **Old Testament Law**?

The thing that **sparked off** Paul's letter was when he heard that the Galatians had been paid a little visit by **the Judaizers**.

They'd basically dumped the Law on the Galatians, telling them they had to get **circumcised**, stop eating **pork**, keep the **sabbath**, etc. Paul was outraged.

Here's how he basically dealt with the issue...

The Law doesn't work – *It's useless trying to please God by keeping all the Old Testament laws. No one could ever do it! This is why Jesus came – to open up a new way to God. To cling to the old laws as a way of putting things right with God is like saying that Jesus died for nothing (Galatians 2:21).*

Your choice: freedom or slavery – *Jesus came to free people from the slavery that sin and guilt bring, says Paul. But submitting to the Law means the Galatians are becoming slaves again. They should learn to value their freedom (see Galatians 5:1).*

The Law vs the Spirit – *Christians receive their power for living a righteous life from God's Spirit. To exchange God's power for your own weak willpower to keep the law is foolish. "You foolish Galatians!" says Paul (see Galatians 3:1–3).*

Freedom to be good – *Towards the end of the letter, Paul gives a warning. Christian freedom from the Law is freedom to do good, and not a licence to behave badly. This is the power of Jesus' good news. It gives people the power to live as God intended (see Galatians 5:22–23).*

You can find one of the most famous moments of the letter in Galatians 5:22–23, where Paul describes the "fruit of the Spirit", beginning with the qualities of love, joy and peace, and ending up with self-control.

EPHESIANS

Ephesus was one of the great cities of the ancient world. It was an **important port** with links to Corinth and Rome. It had its own goddess, **Artemis**, with a temple four times bigger than the Parthenon in Athens. It had a theater seating up to 50,000 people on a good night. And the city boasted a population of one-third of a million people.

The apostle Paul came here around AD 54 and stayed for two years. Read about it in Acts 19.

If Paul was in Ephesus that long, he must have known most of the Christians personally. Yet in his letter to the Ephesians, he doesn't mention anyone by name. How do you explain that?

■ Many experts say Paul **wasn't the author** of Ephesians, partly because of this lack of personal greeting (see page 225).

■ They also believe Ephesians was written not only to the church in Ephesus, but to **a whole group of churches** in the area. The letter would have been passed from church to church (see Colossians 4:16).

Paul (or whoever wrote the letter) starts by saying that the death of Jesus wasn't just some **isolated event** in the backwaters of history. Instead, it was the key ingredient in **God's great plan** for the whole of creation (see Ephesians 1). In Jesus, God **reunites us with God** and with each other by forgiving our sins and setting us free to be his children. Here's how Paul puts it...

This plan is to bring all creation together, everything in heaven and on earth, with Christ as head.

Ephesians 1:10

He then spells out what this means in three ways.

New unity – the death of Jesus reunites people with God and with each other, breaking down the walls which divide people (Ephesians 2:11–22). So Jews and non-Jews now become one in Christ (Ephesians 4:1–16).

New life – the difference between living with and without God is as radical as the dead coming back to life (Ephesians 2:1–10). Paul details the difference this makes in Ephesians 4:17 – 5:20. It means a complete break with the old way of life.

New relationships – this new way of life works out in relationships. Husbands and wives, parents and kids, bosses and workers all have to relate in a new way (Ephesians 5:21 – 6:9). 'Submit to one another,' says Paul.

In a famous New Testament passage, the author compares the struggle to live in this way to a **Roman soldier** dressed for battle (Ephesians 6:10–20).

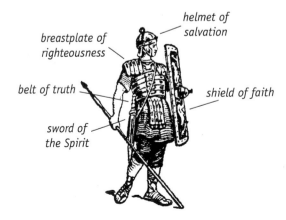

helmet of salvation

breastplate of righteousness

belt of truth

shield of faith

sword of the Spirit

PHILIPPIANS

MACEDONIA

Thessalonica

Philippi

Neapolis

AEGEAN SEA

Philippians is one of the
four New Testament letters
written from prison...

Philemon

Colossians

Philippians

Ephesians

*Traditionally, it's been believed that Paul wrote
Philippians from his captivity in Rome (Acts 28).
However, others think he may have written during his
two-year stretch in Caesarea (Acts 24–26) or from
prison in Ephesus. Wherever Philippians came from,
Paul thought that his execution was very close.*

Paul and the Philippians **went
back a long way.** Right back to
AD 50 in fact, when Paul was on
his second round of travelling.

He hadn't intended to go to
Philippi (the chief city of
Macedonia). But one night he
had **a vision** in which a man
appeared to him and said...

Come over
to Macedonia
and help us!

Acts 16:9

Paul's **earth-shaking** time in
Philippi is recorded in Acts
16:11–40 and makes dramatic
reading. He formed a **close
relationship** with the new
church, especially when they
later helped him through hard
times (see Philippians 4:15–16).

So why did he write to the Philippians?

For **several reasons**...

Note: Write to the Philippians to...

1. say a big thank you for the gifts they sent.

2. tell them how things are in prison – it's not all bad!

3. warn them against the arguments they've been having.

4. alert them to the dangers of the Judaizers (as I did for the Galatians).

5. say that I hope to see them soon.

Any special passages to look out for?

Well, it's all pretty special, but here are three areas...

Philippians 1:20–26 – Paul is torn between wanting to die (to be with Christ) and carrying on the work God's given him to do in this world.

Philippians 2:6–11 – Paul quotes the lyrics of a song (either written by him or by another of the first Christians). The song is a magnificent and yet simply put description of the humiliation and exaltation of Jesus.

Philippians 3:1–11 – Paul attacks the teachers who want Christians to submit to Jewish laws. He writes off his own strict Jewish past as "garbage" compared to knowing Jesus Christ.

Despite the fact that Paul was writing from a potential death-cell, the backbone of his letter is joy. And he calls on his readers to rejoice with him...

Rejoice in the Lord always! I will say it again: Rejoice!

Philippians 4:4

COLOSSIANS

Colossians is an **important letter** in the New Testament, but it has a problem: the experts disagree over whether it was written by Paul or not (see page 225). Leaving that question aside, here's how the letter presents itself.

It all happened something like this...

Pergamum

Sardis

Smyrna

Philadelphia

Ephesus

Laodicea

Colossae

AEGEAN SEA

RHODES

Paul is **in prison** in Rome waiting to be tried. One day, **Epaphras**, a convert of Paul's and a teacher of the church in Colossae, arrives in Rome and brings Paul a mixture of **good news** and **bad news**...

The good news?

And the bad?

The Colossian church is **strong** and **stable**.

A variety of **errors** have crept in. It is these errors which made Epaphras travel the 600 miles to see Paul, and which prompt this letter back to the Colossians.

Put briefly, the **bad report** Epaphras brought was this...

> 1. Some teachers are claiming they have **secret knowledge** of salvation that's **superior** to the teaching given by Paul.
>
> 2. Some teachers also want Christians to adopt Jewish customs such as **circumcision**, following ancient **food laws**, etc...
>
> 3. Others are emphasizing the power of **the spirit world** more than the power of Jesus.

How does the letter **respond**? Paul rightly sees that these teachings attack the central place Jesus Christ has in the salvation of the human race. He counter-attacks by giving his fullest piece of writing on **who Jesus is** and **what he achieved**. The famous passage is in Colossians 1:15–20 and includes the following statements of belief about Jesus Christ...

He is the image of the invisible God...

By him all things were created...

He is the first-born from among the dead...

In him, all things hold together...

All God's fullness dwells in him...

These words of Colossians later became key texts for the church in working out its doctrine of the person of Jesus Christ.

An interesting name crops up at the end of Colossians: **Onesmius** was one of the Christians delivering the letter to Colossae. He was a runaway slave befriended by Paul, and he's the subject of Paul's **letter to Philemon** (page 247).

Philemon
Colossians

1 Thessalonians

Thessalonica was a major city at the time of Paul – and still is today (now called **Salonika**, a fave for Greek holidays). It stood on one of the great east-west Roman roads, and was a natural place for Paul to visit.

So when did Paul go there?

Paul wrote his letter for two main reasons. First, he wanted to encourage the Thessalonians. His letter is warm and full of personal stuff that shows his care and concern.

The Believers
c/o Jason's House
THESSALONICA
Macedonia

Paul also wrote to continue his teaching from where he'd been forced to leave off. The letter is important for its teaching about the second coming of Jesus. See 1 Thessalonians 4:13–18 for the best-known passage.

On his first trip into Greece, Paul visited Thessalonica after he'd been to **Philippi** (Acts 17:1–9). Paul's message polarized his hearers – some were **convinced** while others were **scandalized**.

Mob violence forced Paul to leave the city early – before he'd given the young church the basic teaching it needed to survive in such a hostile place.

He went on to Athens and Corinth, but **Timothy** (Paul's apprentice) went back to Thessalonica. He soon brought Paul news of the church there, which prompted Paul to **write this letter**.

Did you know?

1 Thessalonians is probably the first New Testament letter Paul ever wrote. If so, it would also be the very first bit of the New Testament to have been put on paper.

Letter-writing

Did you know? The New Testament letter-writers didn't write their own letters. Instead, **they dictated** what they had to say to an **amanuensis**, who wrote it all down...

...and the greatest of these is... er...

faith?

The amanuensis wasn't just a **dumb copyist**. He also helped phrase what the writer had to say. Once, Paul's writer signed off himself...

> I, Tertius, the writer of this letter, send you Christian greetings.

And at other times, Paul grabbed the pen himself to finish a letter...

> With my own hand I write this: Greetings from Paul.

THE MAIL

The letters were carried by friends to their destinations. It could take **6–8 weeks** for a letter to reach Philippi from Rome. And a journey from Rome to Jerusalem took just over **3 months**, if the weather was good.

Hmph. The Imperial Post took half the time...

Roman letters of the first century AD didn't start "Dear..." They always began with...

- the **writer's** name
- then the **reader's** name
- then a **greeting**

Paul used the standard Roman opening, but with a strong **Christian emphasis**: "Paul, a prisoner of Christ Jesus... to Philemon... grace to you and peace..." (Philemon 1:1–3).

2 Thessalonians

This letter to the church in Thessalonica was probably not written by Paul, but by a **later author** (see page 225). The author wrote because he'd heard reports that things were **going wrong** for the church. Some of the Thessalonians were saying...

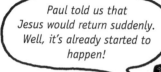

> Paul told us that Jesus would return suddenly. Well, it's already started to happen!

> Fab!

Their confusion over the timing of **the second coming** made the writer respond with some clear, Paul-like teaching on what the second coming would involve. **He said...**

- The return of Christ would be unmistakeable and **cataclysmic**. His vivid description of what it would mean is in 2 Thessalonians 1:7–10.

- Before Christ returns there would be a **worldwide rebellion** against God. This would be led by a mysterious "man of lawlessness". But it couldn't happen yet because a power for good was holding evil in check (2 Thessalonians 2:1–12).

- Meanwhile, the Thessalonian Christians should **work hard** rather than living idle lives (2 Thessalonians 3:6–15).

> ...When the Lord Jesus is revealed from heaven in blazing fire with his powerful angels...

The return of Jesus in 2 Thessalonians 1:7

242

1 Timothy

This letter to Timothy is one of a group of three letters. The backdrop is **the end of Paul's life**, although all three letters were probably written later, by someone else (see page 225).

The letters show that Paul was concerned about what would happen to **the churches** he had cared for over many years. They are written to two of his most trusted assistants, **Timothy** and **Titus**, giving them advice about what they should do.

To: Timothy EPHESUS No.1

To: Titus CRETE

To: Timothy EPHESUS No.2

So, Tim... who was he?

These three letters are known as "the pastoral letters" and are written to church leaders

Timothy was a young man (although probably over 40 when 1 Timothy was written) with a Jewish mother and a Greek father. He became a Christian when Paul visited Lystra, his home town.

The next time Paul passed through he recruited Timothy to join the travelling group (Acts 16:1–5). From then on, Tim was a loyal worker for Paul, mentioned frequently at the end of Paul's letters.

Tim was a bit timid, which explains why 1 and 2 Timothy give him such direct instructions.

1 Timothy concentrates on **three key areas...**

False teaching (chapter 1) – Timothy is told to stand firm.

Life in the church (chapters 2–3) – These chapters focus on worship and church leaders.

Timothy's leadership (chapters 4–5) – The writer finally turns to Timothy with some personal words of advice.

2 Timothy

This letter, which was probably by an unknown author (see page 225), was written as if it was **Paul's final letter...**

Oh no! Is it going to be a weepie?

No. The letter contains words of **thanks**, **encouragement**, **warnings** for the future, **hope** and **joy** – and the writer depicts Paul facing death with no trace of self-pity or complaint about his predicament. He was in prison again in Rome – this time for good. The author says Paul's execution was very near (2 Timothy 4:6).

2 Timothy almost reads like Paul's **last will and testament**. In it the writer gives Paul's final words to Timothy, Paul's **junior partner** in the faith, reminding him of all the two of them had been through together, and telling him how to act as Paul's successor.

The most **stirring passage** comes in chapter 4, where the writer sums up the **heroic** nature of Paul's life and work by saying...

I have fought the good fight, I have finished the race, I have kept the faith. Now there is in store for me the crown of righteousness, which the Lord, the righteous Judge, will award to me on that day...

2 Timothy 4:7–8

THE BIBLE FROM SCRATCH

PAUL

HIS LAST YEARS

What happened to the Apostle Paul? His story seems to end at Acts 28.

The book of Acts tells us that **Paul was arrested** by the Roman authorities in Jerusalem after a riot (Acts 21). As a Roman citizen, he had the **right of appeal** to the **emperor** himself, and when he claimed it, he was sent by ship to Rome (Acts 27).

The book of Acts closes with Paul **under house arrest** in Rome. He lived there for two years in rented accommodation waiting for his trial before the emperor. But then what?

The pastoral letters (1 & 2 Timothy and Titus) give us some information about what might have happened to Paul...

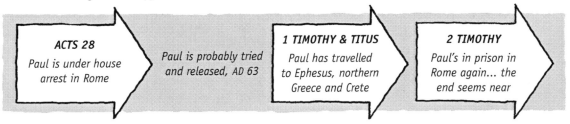

ACTS 28
Paul is under house arrest in Rome

Paul is probably tried and released, AD 63

1 TIMOTHY & TITUS
Paul has travelled to Ephesus, northern Greece and Crete

2 TIMOTHY
Paul's in prison in Rome again... the end seems near

THE END

In AD 64, a **terrible fire** destroyed most of Rome. The Emperor **Nero** was blamed and he needed some scapegoats – fast. He chose the Christians as they were unpopular, and had them put to death in the most cruel ways. It's generally agreed that Paul was a victim of this persecution, put to death **by the sword** around the year AD 67.

THE BIBLE FROM SCRATCH

TITUS

The letter to Titus was written to one of Paul's close companions on **Crete**. Titus was having a **difficult time**. Many Cretans were hot-headed and loved arguments. This was true even of the **church leaders**. The writer of the letter had to say things that ought to go without saying...

A church leader mustn't be arrogant or quick-tempered, or a drunkard, or violent or greedy for money.

Titus 1:7

How had Titus ended up with such a bunch in the first place?

Paul had gone with Titus to Crete when he was **set free** from the imprisonment described in Acts 28. Then Paul left him there to look after the **young church**, while he carried on traveling.

HELP! It looks as if the author of this letter wrote after hearing a **cry for help** from Titus. It seems the Christians on Crete weren't taking him seriously as their leader, so the letter was meant to give Titus some much-needed back-up.

The author uses strong language: Titus is to **sharply rebuke, instruct, urge** and **warn** the church, using his full authority in teaching them. The letter was clearly meant not for Titus' eyes only. It must have strengthened his hand a lot in a hot situation.

Heracleon ■

Crete: no holiday for Titus.

Philemon

This short, personal letter, written by Paul, is about a slave called **Useful**. That's exactly what his master called him (**Onesimus** is the Greek word for "useful").

However, the name was a bit of a joke, because Useful was actually a pretty useless slave. He ended up **stealing** from his master and then **running away.** The punishment for slaves who did this sort of thing was extremely severe.

USEFUL! Bring in the wine, please.

CRASH!

That's another _bottle_ of the Sicilian 22 BC gone...

Slavery

Many churches of that time included slaves and masters. So what did Paul think of slavery?

■ *He told slaves to be good at their slaving! But if they could gain their freedom, they should do so.*

■ *He told masters to treat slaves with humanity.*

■ *Although he didn't come out openly against slavery, he did see it as one of the things Christ had come to destroy (see Galatians 3:28).*

But then **Useful met Paul.** He became a Christian. And at last his life started to match up to his slave name because he became a much-valued companion to Paul in prison. He confessed that he was a runaway slave, and it turned out that his master, **Philemon**, was an old Christian friend of Paul's.

So Paul **sent Useful back** to Philemon, carrying this letter. Paul begged him, in a tactful and humorous way, to...

Well... you can read that for yourself!

HEBREWS

What a strange book! I can't even get beyond verse 4...

Most people who start to read the letter to the Hebrews find it's something of a **foreign book**. That's not surprising since it was written to a particular group of people with special problems. But the message of Hebrews is **amazingly rich**, so it's worth finding out what the writer was aiming to do.

Hebrews was most likely written to **Jewish Christians**. Some writers have suggested that it was written to a **group of priests** from the Jerusalem temple who were converted early on in the book of **Acts**.

Whoever they were, they had been suffering **severe opposition** for their new faith. They were tempted to **give it all up** and return to Judaism.

> **The number of disciples in Jerusalem grew larger and larger, and a great number of priests accepted the faith.**
>
> *Acts 6:7*

All this persecution gives me a headache! Why don't we just go back to our old faith – after all, it's the same God...

The writer of Hebrews responds to this **temptation to de-convert**. Going back to the Jewish faith, he says, is no option. He shows how **Jesus is greater** than the most highly valued aspects of the Jewish faith of the Old Testament...

ANGELS

In the Jewish religion, angels were important messengers sent by God. But Jesus was greater. He was God's Son. His message is also more important (Hebrews 1–2).

MOSES

Moses was a central figure to Judaism – he was given the Law by God on Mt Sinai. But Moses was still only a faithful servant. Jesus was God's Son (Hebrews 3:1–6).

HIGH PRIEST

The Jewish High Priest offered animal sacrifices to pay for the sins of the people. But Jesus was the perfect High Priest because he never committed any sin himself (Hebrews 4: 14 – 7:28). Catholic bishops and priests exercise their special participation in Christ's priesthood while presiding at the eucharist.

SACRIFICES

The Jewish faith relied on an elaborate system of worship in which animals were regularly sacrificed to pay for human sin. Jesus' death was the perfect sacrifice because of who he was, and because he only had to make one sacrifice (Hebrews 9:11–28).

SINAI AGREEMENT

This agreement between God and Israel (the 'Old Testament') was the foundation of the Jewish faith. But it was temporary. Jesus' death has brought the new agreement – "New Testament" – which is permanent (Hebrews 12:18–24).

Don't forget to read chapters 11 and 12. They're inspiring!

Chapters 11 and 12 tell us about the **great cloud of witnesses** – the saints who have gone before us and who show us how to live. They are part of the **communion of saints**. They pray for us and serve as role models as we try to live our lives as saints and witnesses, too.

James

OK, this is the letter of James.

James who?

Well, there's been some **disagreement** about which James we're dealing with. But the earliest view was that the letter was written by James, a **relative of Jesus**. After Jesus' death and resurrection, James became a believer and went on to **lead the church** in Jerusalem. The letter could also have been written by a later admirer of James.

In contrast to Paul's letters, the spotlight in James falls on the **practical issues** facing Christians and the Christian community. The heart of his book is the **vital connection** between faith and action (James 2:14–26). James attacks the kind of faith that believes **one thing** and does **something else**. He sums up his attack by saying...

IN OR OUT?

Some people have questioned whether James should be in the New Testament at all. James is missing from some of the earliest lists of canonical books.

James's most famous critic was Martin Luther (1483–1546), who believed James contradicted Paul's teaching on justification by faith alone. Luther said James was...

an epistle of straw

❝Faith without works is dead.❞ James 2:17

James then goes on to show how this "active faith" works out in practical situations...

The poor (James 2:1–13)

Speaking (James 3:1–12)

Quarrelling (James 4:1–12)

Riches (James 5:1–6)

1 PETER

This letter was written to help Christians prepare themselves for **persecution** by the Roman state. It's one of the **best-loved** New Testament letters, because of its warmth and affection for its readers.

Peter, one of Jesus' first disciples, was said from the earliest times to have written the letter **from Rome**, but modern experts think it may have been written by a later follower of his. Peter is linked with persecution, as he suffered under the first wave of persecution under the sadistic Emperor **Nero**.

> But how did that happen? I thought the Romans were tolerant of Christians at first...

They had been – till now. In July of AD 64, the **great fire of Rome** broke out. Angry crowds blamed Nero, but he pointed the finger at the innocent Christians.

Tacitus, the Roman historian, details the cruel persecution which followed...

They were clad in the hides of beasts and torn to death by dogs; others were crucified, others set on fire to serve to illuminate the night when daylight failed.

Tacitus

This letter was written to Christians in what is now **Turkey**. It's a kind of manual to enable Christians to survive persecution with **their faith intact**.

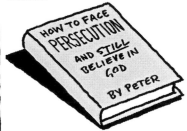

HOW TO FACE PERSECUTION AND STILL BELIEVE IN GOD
BY PETER

Amazingly, the letter is full of **joy**, and in it the writer tells his readers...

■ *You have a living hope. The new life of Jesus gives you strength now, and his second coming gives you hope for the future.*

■ *You suffer in the same way that Jesus did – he is your example.*

■ *You are called to follow Jesus in the way you live, in contrast to the way the rest of the world lives.*

2 PETER

The letter of 2 Peter was **written very late** – many experts date it to around AD 130, fully 100 years after the death of Jesus. This would make it the **last book** of the Bible to be written. The writer was therefore **not Peter**, the disciple of Jesus, but someone who admired Peter enough to write in his name (see page 225 for why authors did this).

There are **two big themes** in the letter.

False teachers

In chapter 2, the writer pours out a fabulous stream of **invective** against false teachers in the church, picturing them as **dogs** returning to their vomit and **sows** "wallowing in the dung". Here's a sample of his style...

> These men are springs without water and mists driven by a storm. Blackest darkness is reserved for them.
>
> *2 Peter 2:17*

The second coming

Chapter 3 of the letter focuses on the promised second coming of Jesus, and deals with the early church's **disappointment** that the second coming was **apparently delayed**. He explains...

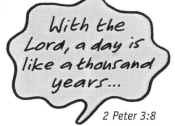

> With the Lord, a day is like a thousand years...
>
> *2 Peter 3:8*

 It looks like the writer of 2 Peter copied a chunk from the book of Jude (virtually all of Jude is repeated in 2 Peter chapter 2)! This is one of the reasons this book was almost rejected from the New Testament.

1,2+3 John

These letters were among **the last letters** of the New Testament to be written. No one knows for sure who wrote them.

1 JOHN
To: Everyone

2 JOHN
To: The Dear Lady and her Children

3 JOHN
To: Gaius, Church Leader

1 John reads more like a tract than a letter. It encourages Christians to love God and each other, and it warns against enemies of the faith.

2 John is a real letter, written with the same aims as 1 John. It is addressed to "The Dear Lady" (a local church), "and her children" (its members).

3 John is a personal note to a church leader, Gaius. It encourages him and warns against a rather proud leader in a nearby church.

So what were these **enemies of the faith** saying?

Listen! I've got some new secret teaching! Everything physical is completely evil... including our bodies. So Jesus wasn't really human as God couldn't become a human with a (yuck!) body. Also... since our bodies are evil anyway, it doesn't matter what we do with them. We can behave as we like!

John answered this (in his first letter) by saying...

- Jesus was a **flesh-and-blood** human. John had heard, seen and touched him (1 John 1:1).
- We must live as God wants, because **God is light** (1 John 1:5–7), not darkness.
- The word which appears again and again in John's letters is **love**. It's at the heart of being a Christian.

God is love
1 John 4:8

Love one another
2 John 5

HEY! JUDE

And who was this Jude?

Like so many of the New Testament letters, Jude was written to attack **false teachers** who had infiltrated the church. (Ironically, heresy has often been valuable to the Christian faith, because it made Jude, John, Paul and other writers define more precisely what they believed.)

Traditionally, he's been identified as a **relative** of Jesus. At the beginning of his letter he identifies himself as "a brother of **James**". But no one really knows who the writer was.

Jude tells us that he was in the middle of writing a longer, more detailed letter setting out the Christian faith, when **bad news arrived.** The false teachers were at it again. So Jude put his longer letter aside and wrote instead a red-hot **denunciation** of the evil teachers.

Jude is perhaps best known for the inspiring **doxology** that closes his book...

Stop the epistle!

To him who is able to keep you from falling and to present you before his glorious presence without fault and with great joy – to the only God our Savior be glory, majesty, power and authority, through Jesus Christ our Lord, before all ages, now and for evermore!
Jude verses 24–25

THE END

You've got to hand it to the Bible for producing a **classy ending.** The final book in the Good Book has a cast of (literally) thousands, choirs of saints and angels, a pitched battle between the forces of **light and darkness**, a smouldering lake of fire for the wicked and paradise regained for the righteous. This means that the Bible begins and ends **with God** and with the promise that the human story, despite its chapters of suffering and despair, will have the ultimate **happy ending.**

The book of Revelation lifts the curtain on what God is doing while the world reels in suffering and horror in the final days of human history. Despite its rather tabloid cast – including the devil and the whore of Babylon – the book has a fabulous grandeur unmatched in the Bible.

REVELATION

The book of Revelation is a type of writing called **apocalyptic**. This Greek word means to **uncover** or **reveal** what was hidden. The book was written by a Christian called John on the Greek island of **Patmos**.

Oh? On vacation, was he?

Unfortunately not. John had been **sent into exile** on Patmos as a punishment for being a Christian. Christians around the empire were being **persecuted**, and the book was written to help them be strong and overcome their trials.

AEGEAN SEA

■ Pergamum
■ Thyatira
Sardis ■
■ Smyrna
Philadelphia
■ Ephesus
Laodicea ■

Patmos

The seven churches of Asia Minor in chapters 1–3

All this led Christians to ask **questions** such as…

The persecution that probably formed the background for John's apocalypse was started by the Emperor Domitian, who ruled from AD 81 to 96. He began to call himself "master and god" and demanded people worship him. Those who refused were seen as traitors and faced the possibility of being put to death. Many Christians suffered and died for their faith at this time.

Why is evil triumphing over goodness?

Will we all be wiped out?

How long before God does something?

John's apocalypse was a **direct response** to the confusion, doubt and despair of many Christians. It came to him in a series of **bizarre visions**, which are in the same "family" as the visions in the Old Testament books of **Daniel** and **Zechariah**.

So how did the book help these persecuted Christians?

John's visions let us see a glimpse **behind the scenes** of history. Although there is a mighty clash between the forces of good and evil, God is the **absolute ruler** of all that goes on.

Rome and its evil may seem to be in control, the book says, but put your trust in God, the **King of kings** and **Lord of lords**.

This list of **the main characters** in the book gives an idea of what John's visions are like, and may help in finding your way around…

THE LAMB
Symbolizes Jesus, who gave up his life as a sacrifice (chapters 5, 14 and 19)

THE FOUR HORSE RIDERS
They bring conquest, war, famine and death (chapter 6)

SEVEN ANGELS WITH SEVEN TRUMPETS
Each trumpet-blast heralds God's judgment (chapters 8–11)

THE WOMAN GIVING BIRTH
She represents God's people, and her child is the messiah (chapter 12)

THE DRAGON
Has seven heads and ten horns – this is Satan (chapters 12 and 20)

THE BEASTS OF EARTH AND SEA
Symbolize anti-God powers and authorities (chapter 13)

SEVEN ANGELS WITH SEVEN PLAGUES
These plagues are like the ones in Exodus (chapters 15–16)

THE WHORE OF BABYLON
She symbolizes the city of Rome – but every era has its own 'Babylon' (chapters 17–18)

THE BRIDE
She is the opposite of the whore of Babylon and represents the church (chapter 19)

THE RIDER OF THE WHITE HORSE
This is the Son of God in his great power (chapter 19)

The book closes in chapters 21 and 22 with a vision of a **new heaven and earth**. These chapters dramatically describe the completion of God's work in Jesus, with the re-creation of a world that was spoiled by human sin.

the 7 churches

John addressed the book of Revelation to **seven churches** in the Roman province of Asia (today's western Turkey – see the map on page 238). The first three chapters of Revelation contain seven **mini-letters**, each one addressed to one of the seven churches.

SEA MAIL
To: Churches at Ephesus, Smyrna, Pergamum, Thyatira, Sardis, Philadelphia and Laodicea

John has a special message from God for all seven churches. Each mini-letter has the same **structure**...

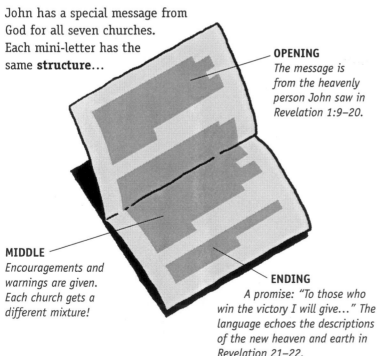

OPENING
The message is from the heavenly person John saw in Revelation 1:9–20.

MIDDLE
Encouragements and warnings are given. Each church gets a different mixture!

ENDING
A promise: "To those who win the victory I will give..." The language echoes the descriptions of the new heaven and earth in Revelation 21–22.

So what's in these letters?

The seven churches, at the end of the first century AD, were facing **many problems**, including false apostles, pagan religions, emperor worship and persecution. Plus **internal problems**: cooling of love for God, apathy and immorality. The churches receive sharply worded **warnings** about it all.

UNDERSTANDING IT

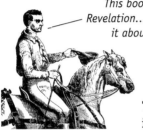

This book of Revelation... what's it about?

The book of Revelation is notoriously hard to understand. Is it written in code? Does it give us a date for the end of the world? Who is the Antichrist? What on earth is it all about? Here are three friendly bits of advice to help you get started on the message of this great-but-strange book...

1 Start with the past

Start by looking at the book through the eyes of its first readers. This is true for any part of the Bible. So remember that Revelation's first readers were persecuted and looking for encouragement. They would see references to Rome and its hoped-for destruction throughout the book.

2 Go on to the future

Revelation looks forward to the end of time – so it's not just about the fall of ancient Rome. God's judgment on the Roman empire is a picture of what he will do to all evil powers, past, present and future. Two levels of prophecy are at work here: one is about the fall of Rome; while the second level is about the fall of the evil that inspired Rome.

3 Don't trip up over details

Some authors try to find modern meanings for the tiniest details in the book, while others use it to pin a date on the second coming. It's best to avoid this sort of thing like the plague. Revelation isn't a code book, waiting to be cracked.

THE BIBLE FROM SCRATCH

your notes.

your notes.

your notes.

your notes.

THE END